Benchmarks of Quality in the Church

Benchmarks of Quality in the Church:

21 Ways to Continuously Improve the Content of Your Ministry

Norman Shawchuck & Gustave Rath

Abingdon Press
Nashville

BENCHMARKS OF QUALITY IN THE CHURCH

This book is printed on recycled, acid-free paper.

Library of Congress Cataloging-in-Publication Data

Rath, Gustave J.
    Benchmarks of quality in the church : 21 ways to continuously
improve the content of your ministy / Gustave J. Rath and Norman
Shawchuck.
        p.   cm.
    Includes bibliographical references and index.
    ISBN 0-687-34912-5   (pbk. : alk. paper)
        1. Clergy—Office.   2. Pastoral theology.   3. Christian
    leadership. I. Shawchuck, Norman, 1935–   . II. Title.
BV660.2.R35   1994
254—dc20   94-18071
                                                                              CIP

Unless otherwise noted, Scripture quotations are from the New Revised Standard Version Bible, Copyright 1989 by the Division of Christian Education of the National Council of the Churches of Christ in the USA. Used by permission.

Those noted NIV are from the Holy Bible, New International Version®. Copyright © 1973, 1978, 1984 by International Bible Society. Used by permission of Zondervan Publishing House.

94 95 96 97 98 99 00 01 02 03 — 10 9 8 7 6 5 4 3 2 1

MANUFACTURED IN THE UNITED STATES OF AMERICA

Contents

Acknowledgments

This book is dedicated to important persons in my life who most modeled Quality in all their doings. Their examples have encouraged and assisted my own quest for quality.

To Mary Ann Mueller, Donna Waters Wood, Shirley Teare, Diane Sinnish and Jacqueline Bauer—office colleagues whose total commitment to the highest quality in their work has made the offices in which we worked productive, enjoyable and, sometimes, sane.

To my teachers: Margorie Zeller, my first-grade teacher who held my hand while I struggled to do the "ovals"; Alvin Lindgren, whose teaching inspired me to become a teacher; Gustave Rath, whose superior intellect and teaching abilities continually challenge me to never settle for what I already know; Peter F. Drucker, who has perhaps taught me more about leadership and organization than any other teacher.

To A. James Armstrong, Robert Paul, Rueben Job, Ron Hartung and Bruce Ough, who gave me my first opportunity to serve on a learning team the Dakotas Area Program Staff of The United Methodist Church. Because of them, I can always say I once served on a true learning team.

To John Wagner, Colin Brown and Chuck Adkins, my colleagues while we served the First United Methodist Church in Michigan City, Indiana—for too short a time. Because of them I can say I served on learning teams twice in my life—a rare gift for anyone working in religious institutions.

To Larry Dalton, a volunteer layperson in Michigan City, Indiana, whose vision, courage and sacrifice brought into being The Open Door, a free clinic of the highest quality that was nominated as one of President George Bush's Thousand Points of Light.

To Bishop David Lawson, Susan Ruach, Sam Phillips and Elvin Miller, with whom I worked in the Indiana Area, United Methodist Church. Their commitment to quality in spiritual formation lifted the spirit of the Church in Indiana. Elvin Miller's career-long com-

7

mitment to quality continuing education for clergy resulted in perhaps the finest judicatory training program for pastors in the United States.

To Bishop Dale White, whose personal integrity, unwavering dedication to social justice and to quality ministry has been a constant inspiration and model.

To Paul Franklyn, Linda Allen and John Robinson, the Abingdon Team whose commitment to quality in professional publications gives the constant assurance that they will not let my work pass until it is done well.

To Carita Shawchuck, Melody Shawchuck and Kay Shawchuck Abdullah, my daughters, whose dedication to their education and professional careers has led them to the heights Verna and I dreamed of when first we held them, each one, in our arms.

To Verna Shawchuck, my partner in living for thirty-eight years, whose indomitable drive for excellence in all that she does has set the standard in quality for our daughters and myself.

To my mother, Ava, who made me learn and recite poetry from age four, and my father, Alexander Nickita, who gave me my love for books. From this springs my love affair with words in every form. Without this my life would be immensely deprived.

To Robert Worley, Roger Heuser and Wayne Purintun, each committed to the highest standards in their private and professional lives. Words are insufficient to express my appreciation and debt to these colleagues.

To my students WhaJa Hwang, Kee Woo Kang, Chip Johnson, Leon Finney and Riad Jajour, who took our meager wares and transformed them into quality ministries that span the world.

To Makram Mehany, friend and brother, whose commitment to Christ and the church in the Middle East has resulted in a small-group movement across the Middle East and then allowed Verna and me to have a small part in it.

To these and many more men and women who have instructed, inspired and challenged me to seek quality in all that I do, I dedicate this book, my friendship and service.

Norm Shawchuck

I wish to dedicate this book to those who helped me come to this place in my life:

To my mother, Margaret Rose Payor Rath, for encouraging and guiding me into the life of the ivy-covered college.

To my wife, Karen Sue Stoyanoff, who has filled my life, especially relevant since she enrolled in theological school.

To my close friends and intellectual companions with whom I have spent interminable hours talking: Philip Kotler and Norman Shawchuck.

To Northwestern University, which has given me the freedom to pursue many occupations during my life.

To my students from Northwestern University and Garret-Evangelical Theological Seminary, who keep me alive and thinking.

To the many denominations, judicatories, and churches with whom I have had the privilege to consult as well as learn from.

To Paul Franklyn, who believed in and contributed much to our project, and Linda Allen, who is again giving us editorial support.

Gus Rath

Preface

Gustave is an industrial engineer. In his younger days Norman was a survey party crew chief in civil engineering. As such the word "benchmark" is significant to us. We have chosen to use it in this book even though it may not be as familiar to our readers. We do this because the word, *benchmark*, says so succinctly what we are trying to convey about the Qualities discussed in this book.

A benchmark is an established point either to take off from, or to return to. A benchmark is a point of reference for measuring distances, elevations, attitudes or actions. For example, the topography of the United States has a benchmark. It is called "sea level" and is established at 0.00 feet. The highest point in the United States is Mt. McKinley, Alaska at 20,321.00 feet above sea level. On the other hand, the lowest point in the United States is Death Valley, CA. at −282.00 feet below the United States Geological benchmark for sea level. Benchmarks are also established to indicate exactly where a certain point is relative to longitude and latitude.

The Qualities discussed in this book may serve as benchmarks to help you assess your church's position relative to being a "total quality" congregation. Of course, it is possible to stretch our benchmark metaphor to the point where it begins to break down. Within reasonable boundaries, however, it is illuminating and appropriate to consider the Qualities discussed herein as benchmarks to help you determine where you might most helpfully put time and attention to move your church further along the road toward becoming a quality operation. Each Quality is a point of reference for you to start from, or to return to, in working with groups, and doing your own work.

This book discusses twenty-one Qualities. It may not be possible for you to put attention to all of them at once. You will want to select those Qualities thoughtfully, which you believe may have the most systemic effects upon your total church programs. Begin by conducting a congregation evaluation, or listening process, to ascertain which of the Qualities seem most in need of attention, or offer ready promise for quick improvement—and begin your journey toward greater quality from that vantage point.

Why Quality Is So Important

As we finish our work on this book, one of the major topics in the corporate world is the Bell Atlantic-TCI megamerger, and the anticipation of even more awesome breakthroughs in the world of telecommunications. In late October 1993 the giants of the multimedia industry met in Washington to discuss the mergers and the future of their enterprise. The October 21, 1993, issue of *USA Today* carried a brief report of the meeting, written by Kevin Maney:

> They're stunned at the speed of . . . technological change. "I don't think any of us envisioned the kind of megadeals we're seeing today," Sculley said. . . . "The pace will pick up. . . . Decisions will have to have been made by the end of 1994 or you'll find you're too far back of the starting line." MCI's Roberts said. . . . "The question is not whether big or small is better. The issue in this new economic age is quality, not size." Brown said.

This book is about *Quality* for religious organizations. We believe this to be a timely topic because several of the statements quoted above are as true for the church as they are for the telecommunications industry. Rapid change is affecting not just the megachurches, but the smaller churches as well. Large or small, the only churches to survive will be those that make *Quality* the standard in all that they do. In the church, as in the telecommunications world of information that now dominates our society, the issue is quality, not size.

Congregations do not have much time to think about this matter. Religious researchers are already predicting that 60 percent of the congregations now in existence will be closed by the year 2050. Will your congregation be among this number? You will have to make decisions about this now—or you will be too far behind the starting line to survive the changes that are already pressing in upon your church, whether you know it or not.

This book is directed toward a discussion of the content of quality in congregations—the areas in which the congregation must achieve high-quality performance if it is to do well. We will list twenty-one

Qualities. Only a few congregations will likely possess the resources to begin working on all of the Qualities at once. If your congregation is not one of those lucky few, then pick out one or two of those Qualities toward which there is the greatest openness in your church—and go to work. To effect change in some of the areas will create the conditions for greater openness in the others.

Thinking About Quality

> Quality: Doing things right! Doing them right the first time. Striving to do things better today than we did yesterday, and keeping at it until we exceed being the best, and set our sights on the highest goal of all—perfection.

If you are hesitant about discussing quality from the perspective of culture, or the secular business world, then you ought to be pondering, "What might God think about Quality as a consideration for church leaders and congregations?" When we consider God's thoughts (if we can do so in a reasonable manner), we will be doing theology. At a very basic level theology is an attempt to think about things as God may think about them.

Now, the very idea that we might be able to think as God thinks is blatantly arrogant and overly ambitious for our limited capacities. So, we should only do it playfully, as children; remembering that to children play is serious, and it stimulates growth.

JESUS AS A MODEL OF QUALITY IN MINISTRY

By any standard, Jesus' ministry was a work to be imitated. Whatever else one may say about the ministry of Jesus, one must admit he did it with Quality. We read the Gospels and marvel at how he seemed always to have the right word, the critical insight needed to understand and help people. And he was able to perform his acts of ministry in a manner that often amazed even his harshest critics.

Dallas Willard, in his book *The Spirit of the Disciplines*, muses on the reasons why Jesus might have been so successful in his public ministry and concludes that Jesus was only able to "perform on the spot" in his public ministry because of the relationship he kept with God in his private life.[1] Jesus sustained a rhythm in his life of going from public ministry to solitude and prayer, and of coming to public ministry out of solitude and prayer. Henri Nouwen also makes a clear connection between one's ministry and one's spirituality, asserting that a ministry that is not undergirded by spirituality will wither:

> Ministry is service in the name of the Lord. Spirituality is attention to the life of the Spirit in us.
> We have fallen into the temptation of separating ministry from spirituality, service from prayer. Our demon says: "We are too busy to pray; we have too many needs to attend to, too many people to respond to, too many wounds to heal. Prayer is a luxury, something to do during a free hour, a day away from work or on a retreat." But to think this way is harmful. Service and prayer can never be separated; they are related to each other as the Yin and Yang of the Chinese Circle.[2]

Ministry consumes energy. Spirituality restores energy. We all know this, and yet we resist it. Consequently we wander about in our ministries with our fuel gauges on empty, blaming God for our inability to "perform on the spot," our inability to heal the many people who come our way, or to turn our fading dreams into vivid reality. Some of us have wandered far astray from the recognition that the Reformers had of the inextricable influence our private lives have upon the quality of our public ministry, the influence of our spirituality upon the quality of our efforts.

Why should we put such emphasis upon our interior, mystical lives, when our call is to minister to persons and situations in externally oriented and concrete situations? Carlo Carretto, in his book *Letters to Dolcidia*, confides that he struggled with this question for years: working hard, becoming a famous priest in Europe, heading the Catholic Youth Workers Movement—only one day to hear God calling him to lay it all down and to go to the Algerian desert to be with the Little Brothers of Jesus; there to spend many years in desert solitude and prayer. Always, he says, he asked why. Why should he leave a very public ministry that was far above average in results to spend these mounting years in the desert? Then, after ten years he heard God say, "Carlo, old boy, it's not your work that I want. I want you."[3]

The first Quality God looks for in our ministry is a quality relationship between ourselves and God. The Quality of this relationship affects all the other qualities in our work. Without high-quality relationship with God, one will be a trifler in work and ministry. Without vision there is no quality; only unfocused, and often fretful, activity and vision is gestated in the womb of one's relationship with God. Without vision the people perish. Without vision the ministry will perish. Without vision *the minister* perishes.

The Reformers and Quality

The Reformers were probably almost as busy as we, yet their response to the daily grind was an inversion of our values and attitudes. And so Luther said, "I am so busy and burdened with these mounting responsibilities that unless I pray four hours a day I won't get my work done." Later John Wesley wrote to a pastor of a small congregation who complained that Wesley was expecting too much by way of study and prayer: "Oh, begin! Set some time each day for prayer and Scripture whether you like it or not. It is for your life! Else you will be a trifler all your days."

Even before the Reformers Luther and Wesley, that great Reformer St. Paul urged Quality as the ultimate standard by which we should measure the small and large tasks, and the services which God sets before us each day:

> By the grace God has given me, I laid a foundation as an *expert builder,* and someone else is building on it. But each one should be careful how he [or she] builds. . . . His [or her] work will be shown for what it is, because the Day will bring it to light. It will be revealed with fire, and the fire will test the quality of each [one's] work. (1 Cor. 3:10, 13 NIV; italics added)

> *Do your best* to present yourself to God as one approved, a workman who does not need to be ashamed. (2 Tim. 2:15 NIV; italics added)

Whatever you do, *work at it with all your heart*, as working for the Lord. (Col. 3:23 NIV; italics added).

Indeed the Scriptures and the Reformers have much to say about Quality. If Paul is correct, the quality of our work (not only our faith or morals) will be tested, and some will be approved while others will be ashamed. Small wonder, then, that Paul should encourage us to work at our tasks with all our hearts, to do *high-quality work*, because we are working for the Lord: "The work of each builder will become visible . . . because it will be revealed with fire, and the fire will test [the quality] of work each has done. If what has been built on the foundation survives, the builder will receive a reward. If the work is burned up, the builder will suffer loss" (1 Cor. 3:13-15).

Quality—ministry. For decades the North American church has hardly believed that there was any reason why these two words should go together. "After all," some might say, "we're doing this for the church. So what if it ain't so hot? As long as we're dedicated, anything is good enough for the church." Or perhaps you've heard, "God looks upon the heart, not upon the quality of our choir, or our Sunday school classes. So long as our volunteers are dedicated, it doesn't matter whether they are singing in the right register."

It may not matter to us, but the Scriptures insist that it matters to God. And furthermore, *dedicated incompetency is still incompetency.*

What does it mean to do our work as though we were working for the Lord? Does it not mean that whatever little part we play in the drama of bringing God's Word and Way to the world is terribly important in God's estimation, and we should do it with great care because God is our supervisor to whom we report daily?

By now someone may be saying, "Come now, God accepts our unprepared lessons and our off-key choirs and the broken-down cribs in our nursery and the weather-beaten sign and the unkept lawn. After all, God accepts us just the way we are." Yes, perhaps, if you insist on trivializing God's acceptance so that it applies to sloppiness. But the conversation should not end there, for even if God can excuse poor quality, the "thirty-something" generation (the very generation we must reach if our congregations are to still be around in the year 2025) has already proven that it will not—neither in education for their children, nor in dish-washing soap, and certainly not in religion.

Consider the young couples who regularly utilize the services of more than one congregation. For example, we recently interviewed a couple in Georgia who told us that they and their children begin their Sunday routine by attending the first half of the worship service at a local Baptist church, and then rush down the street to hear the preaching at a United Methodist church, and to deliver their children to the United Methodist Sunday school—because the music program at the Baptist church is superior while the preaching and Sunday school at the United Methodist church is better than at the Baptist church.

Lyle Schaller finds this sort of search for Quality in religious services to be a growing phenomenon. In *The Seven-Day-A-Week Church*, Schaller says, "One way that some churches have become very large congregations is by attention to detail and quality. . . . Quality and attention to detail encourage many first time visitors to return."[4] Furthermore, the Lily Endowment states that baby boomers feel free to pick and choose a denomination and a congregation, and many boomers *shop* for a church that will meet their needs.[5]

Quality is a lesson that North American industry has been slow to learn. All Americans are paying the price for their learning disability. The price can be measured today in such things as the "unbalance" balance of payments, the tremendous advance of Japanese products into America, and the unemployment lines in every city and hamlet. Around 1960 when the Japanese attained 1 percent of the American market, American automobile companies thought these cars were a joke. When the Japanese gained 5 percent of the market by 1965, Detroit brushed it aside, denying that it was a problem. By 1970 when Japanese autos took 10 percent of the market, they were wondering how they could compete. They wondered whether more aggressive selling and tricks (such as cash rebates or 2 percent interest gimmicks) would stop the loss of business. But by the time the Japanese had gained 15 percent of the American market, only a complete turnaround would save the industry. The decline continued until 1985 when the Japanese had 30 percent of the market.[6] Up until this time, however, the American automobile industry actually believed that the American buyer valued style and size more than quality. So long as the car was pretty and large, the American buyer would pay for poor quality—and they were wrong.

The North American companies built cars to make money, while the Japanese built cars to make satisfied customers. But even the American giants could not forever ignore the interests of the customer. Slowly, begrudgingly, the concept of Quality was allowed a place upon the North American scene. Today there is hardly a company in America that does not have a Quality Program, Total Quality Management, or a Performance Improvement Effort.

Generally the church lags behind the changes in its environment by about twenty or thirty years. The respect for tradition is so strong and the fear of acculturation so pervasive that the environment more often represents a threat than an opportunity. But with respect to Quality the American church has been a pacesetter. At least two decades before American industry began to think about Quality, a growing number of pastors and churches had made Quality the norm for everything they do—from the parking lot greeters to the choir and sermon, from the Sunday school classroom to the way the ruling board conducts its business.

And why not? Is not the mission of the church worthy of our best effort? And have not the Scriptures urged Quality upon us for at least three thousand years?[7] Indeed, we write on Quality not because Quality is something the church and its leaders should consider, but because we discover that pastors and churches are already thinking about it. We write this book in the hope that it might add stimulus and focus to the quest for Quality that the American pastors and congregations have already begun.

Quality in the church begins with the leaders' relationship with God. Our spirituality has tremendous effect upon the quality of our ministry in all of its aspects. Oh, begin—else you will be a trifler all your days!

Removing the Barriers to Growth and Quality

The standards of quality and the desire for church growth are not directly related. We would be reluctant to write a book on church growth, because we think it addresses the matter of growth from the wrong angle. Focusing on church growth is very much like dieting to lose weight: If you go on a diet and stick to it, you will lose weight. But when the dieter goes off the diet, the weight will tend to creep back—because the dieter focused on the diet and not on the habits that caused the weight gain in the first place. Almost any reasonable diet will work in the short run, but virtually all diets fail in the long run because losing weight is a systemic issue. There is much more to it than cutting out candy bars and grits for a month.

Similarly, increasing attendance and the scope of ministry of a church is a systemic matter. If a congregation attempts to grow by pressing for growth, it will likely achieve growth for a while. But attempting to grow by focusing on growth will later create unwanted effects that will retard growth and ultimately reverse the growth pattern. In the language of systems theory, which borrows the image of a power saw, attempting to expand by trying to get more people will eventually "kick back."

Two congregations in the same denomination both had pastors who decided to focus on growth by pushing growth, but without removing the key barriers to growth. One of the congregations was located in the conservative East, and the other in the Bible Belt of the South. In both instances each congregation grew very rapidly until reaching about one thousand in attendance, then turned back toward decline. One church exploded into decline, losing some 700 people almost overnight. The other church suddenly stopped growing and within one year had lost the total number of persons added during the growth phase.

The barriers to enduring growth were the same in both instances. First, the pastors had a clear vision of the possibilities, but each failed to communicate the vision to his existing congregation. One pastor announced the vision once but then failed to persuade the people to support it. Both pastors failed to inform the congregation of major programs and changes intended to push growth, so that when the programs and changes were launched, they took the congregations by complete surprise. In one of the congregations the element of complete surprise and the huge success of the efforts literally blew the existing congregation away—several hundred left within a few weeks.

Perhaps the most famous example in Pentecostal circles is the history of a pastor who has taken two different congregations with only a handful of people to several thousand in a very few years. Then, when he left, each congregation plummeted to about 250 people within a year or so.

These are vivid examples of what can be expected, although usually in not such dramatic fashion, when the leaders of a congregation fail to recognize that growth is a systemic issue.

The principle we are discussing here might be stated as:

Don't push growth; remove the factors limiting growth.[8]

Focusing on Quality Will Remove Many Barriers to Growth

A church demographer recently said in a private conversation that he expects that 60 percent of the American Protestant churches in existence today will no longer exist by the year 2050. On the other hand, there are many small congregations today, and also many large ones, that will be around in 2050 because they are learning how to use Quality as a standard for removing the barriers to continuous renewal. *Learning* is the right word here—because Quality can be learned. It is astonishing how quickly churches can learn about Quality—when it is effectively taught. Looking at many learning congregations, and writing about them, has led us to find some of the excellent, successful or model churches in the United States.[9]

Don't push growth; remove the factors limiting growth.

In the early 1980s one of the authors (Shawchuck) was privileged to join with the South Indiana Conference, United Methodist Church, in an experiment of training the pastors of twenty-two very small, isolated congregations nestled away in the hill country along the Ohio River. The memberships of these congregations ranged from six to thirty members. The pastors of these congregations knew that these churches would never be very large. Growth was not the goal; Quality in ministry was. Under the capable leadership of their district superintendent, Sam Phillips, these pastors covenanted together to move their congregations from a survival mentality to a quest for Quality.

By the end of this nine-month experiment, each of these congregations had been transformed by a newfound vision of Quality in their services and in their ministries to their communities. The pastors also experienced transformation, as attested by the fact that they remained in covenant, meeting regularly to support one another.

An example of what these congregations learned about Quality is the United Methodist church in Elizabeth, Indiana, a congregation then numbering 25 members. Elizabeth's claim to fame derived from becoming the weekend meeting place for hundreds of bikers who gathered there to party, exchange drugs, and otherwise infuriate the residents. Under the guidance of their pastor, the congregation decided to stop hating these bikers who terrorized their town and to start loving them in a quality fashion. But how?

They found the answer under the leadership of a young couple who decided to show hospitality to the bikers by opening a hospitality center for them. Soon the members of the defunct Presbyterian congregation joined in this bold effort. Together these folk refurbished the abandoned Presbyterian church building and opened it to the bikers as a show of friendship. And after a while many of the bikers joined them in friendship.

The first biker to enter the hospitality center was soon convinced that their Lord and Savior might also become his Lord and Savior. The community then sent this young man through a drug counselor training program. He returned to Elizabeth to establish a successful counseling program in the hospitality center. This congregation did not grow in membership, but it did learn the essence of Quality in ministry.

In recent years "megachurches" (congregations of several thousand people) are attracting attention. The very large church is a recent phenomenon in our country, and far different from the older Sunday-morning churches that served the Protestant establishment. We are often asked: "How does one become a megachurch?" As we have pondered this question, we conclude that the founders (such as Bill Hybels, Robert Schuller, and Rick Warren) never set out to create megachurches. Megachurches are the product of doing things right—for the Christ whom they are seeking to serve to the best of their abilities. We have witnessed the results of this quest for Quality in large and small churches. Thus, we began speaking and writing of the high-quality church.

The Content of Quality (vs. the Process of Quality)

Much is written today regarding the *process* of Quality Management. This body of material falls under several rubrics, the best known being Total Quality Management (TQM). TQM deals with the management process for achieving quality. TQM assumes that if the institution can master the process of quality, then the content of quality (what quality comprises) will be automatically achieved. This may be true for the manufacturing industry, which, given any product, is designed to mass produce it. However, we think that the content of quality is not clearly apparent for religious organizations. In a surprising reversal of conventional wisdom, we think that if a church leader (and in particular a pastor) understands the content of Quality, he or she will likely find the right process for making Quality happen in the church.

Members of a congregation also need to know what Qualities can be achieved in their church. An understanding of the *content* of quality is thus crucial to everyone in the congregation. We propose, therefore, to set forth twenty-one benchmarks of quality by which a congregation can measure the content of its ministry.

We provide an introduction to the applicable process ideas of TQM in the appendix of this book. And, to overcome cultural resistance, we have translated TQM ideas specifically for church use. Even as we write this book, we are aware that other authors are preparing manuscripts on Total Quality Management for congregations. We have included references to several useful resources on TQM for the reader who wishes to study the subject further.

In this book we identify six groupings or sets of qualities and list the qualities that make up each group—a total of twenty-one benchmarks. The sets into which we have gathered the qualities are not important. The qualities are important and stand on their own quite apart from the groups into which we have gathered them.

The qualities are interdependent; each quality supports all of the others. In other words, the qualities are contagious—each one has a systemic effect upon the entire effort of the congregation. Our experience in working with hundreds of churches, however, convinces us that the religious qualities (spirituality, believing, vision led, mission driven, discerning) and the expecting qualities (ethical, has high expectations, excellence, evaluative) are of primary importance, in that they establish the standards or benchmarks and provide the energy for all of the others. We might diagram the qualities as follows:

Figure 1
Qualities for a Religious Organization

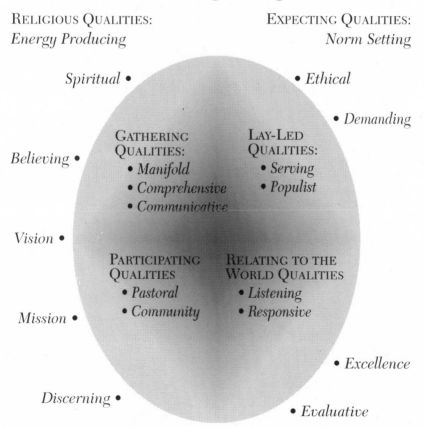

RELIGIOUS QUALITIES:
Energy Producing

EXPECTING QUALITIES:
Norm Setting

Spiritual •

• *Ethical*

• *Demanding*

Believing •

GATHERING QUALITIES:
• *Manifold*
• *Comprehensive*
• *Communicative*

LAY-LED QUALITIES:
• *Serving*
• *Populist*

Vision •

PARTICIPATING QUALITIES
• *Pastoral*
• *Community*

RELATING TO THE WORLD QUALITIES
• *Listening*
• *Responsive*

Mission •

• *Excellence*

Discerning •

• *Evaluative*

1 - Religious Qualities

RELIGIOUS QUALITY IS THE MEANS BY WHICH A CONGREGATION RENEWS ITSELF AND FINDS THE ENERGY TO CARRY OUT AN EFFECTIVE MINISTRY.

➡ SPIRITUALITY
➡ BELIEVING
➡ VISION LED
➡ MISSION DRIVEN
➡ DISCERNING

F ive primary qualities combine to characterize the ability and desire of the church leaders to integrate the espoused faith stance of the congregation with the church's daily life. These benchmark qualities include the *spirituality and the spiritual formation* of its members, the attention the leaders give to teaching and modeling *the vital doctrines,* the *vision* that the congregation holds of its future and its resulting understanding of its *mission* and the *decision-making processes* used to make major decisions about ministry.

➡ RELIGIOUS QUALITIES
➡ SPIRITUALITY

➡ DEFINITION   The benchmark of Spirituality includes embarking on a spiritual journey, adopting spiritual practices, sharing the journey with others and doing good deeds. The pastor(s) publicly affirms this spiritual journey, assists in forming the spirituality of others and supports spiritual activities. Spiritual formation in the nature of Christ is a combination of cognitive learnings and heart-felt experiences. In this benchmark effort the pastor and church leaders take a public stance.

➡ EXAMPLES **A pastor puts spiritual formation at the top of his priorities for the congregation.** The authors have a friend who, upon becoming the pastor of a congregation, preached his first sermon titled, "My Spiritual Journey." He followed this personal saga with a four-sermon series on the spiritual journey and spiritual formation. During these five weeks several persons approached him to teach a class on the subject.

He responded by teaching a twelve-week session on "Steps to a Deeper and More Satisfying Christian Life." He planned the class sessions to allow thirty minutes of instruction on one of the Means of Grace and on the vital doctrines, as taught by John Wesley. Following the instruction period he allowed thirty minutes during which the class divided into small groups to discuss the material he presented as it might apply to their own lives.[1]

He also conducted three spiritual formation retreats throughout his first year at the church. The first two retreats were held in the church building, running from Friday evening until 4:30 P.M. on Saturday. About twenty-five persons attended each of these retreats. The third retreat was held at a retreat center, beginning Friday evening and ending at 3:00 P.M. on Sunday. Seventy persons attended this retreat.

He encouraged all of the interested retreatants to continue meeting in small *covenant groups* on a three-month experimental basis. Virtually all of the retreat participants entered into the three-month covenant group experience. Most of these groups continued for several years and became the nuclei for many spiritual initiatives and social ministries, some of which attained statewide attention for the ministries that they performed in the community.

A congregation adopts spiritual formation as its mission. Tim Jones, Presbytery Executive of the Maumee Presbytery in Ohio, recently told us an exciting story about a congregation that made a bold commitment to focus on spiritual formation.

The congregation is now fourteen years old. It started with thirty-five members and grew to 450 people in two years, and stayed at that plateau for twelve years. It was a strong church, but nothing new or vital happened. At the beginning of their fifteenth year the Session (the congregation's leadership board) called upon the congregation to enter into a discernment process to discover a new vision for the church. The congregation decided that the church should become a place where people could come for spiritual development. This decision caused fifteen members to leave the church, but within a short time seventy-five new persons joined the church upon hearing that the congregation had decided to focus upon spiritual formation.

The congregation has now trained seventy-five of its members to offer spiritual direction and to conduct guided retreats. To be a member of this congregation, one must commit to participating in two spiritual life retreats a year, and also to be guided by a spiritual director. All but thirty of the members are under spiritual direction. The congregation has become alive and vital in all its ministries.

➡ COMMENTS   Spirituality, like Christian education or the church's financial affairs, requires specific skills, organizational structure and leadership. Each congregation, much like General Motors or the League of Women Voters, has its own "spirit." The congregation may be mean-spirited, timid, fearful, friendly, and so on. Spirit is the sense of vitality and vision which is at the heart of the congregation. Some congregations are more vision-led and mission-driven than others. These drives are greatly influenced by the spirituality and spiritual formation (or lack of it) that is fostered in the congregation. The pastor and leaders who merely assume the presence of a vital spirituality will do so to their ultimate regret. Spirituality is not to be assumed; rather, it must be defined, nurtured, and attended.

➡ DIAGNOSTIC QUESTIONS   At the end of each discussion of a particular benchmark quality, we will present a series of diagnostic questions. The questions are offered to assist the reader to reflect upon the condition of each quality in his or her own church. Observing other congregations can often suggest models and ideas for one's own church. You should be ready to expand the lists of questions with some of your own, and to generate some ideas that might be applied in your particular situation. Each congregation should set its own standards and measures. So, please feel free to be creative in using and interpreting these questions.

Consider these questions dealing with the quality of spirituality and spiritual formation:

Do the congregation's leaders publicly witness to their own spiritual journeys? Two questions need to be answered: Who are the leaders? How will we check to see whether they are giving public witness to the means by which they are nurturing their own spiritual growth? Obviously, the pastor(s), staff and board members (trustees, etc.) are among the designated congregational leaders. Others may be long-term members, committee heads and some more recent members. Clearly, it is easy to monitor public services or meetings to see whether such sharing is happening. However, what are other settings and vehicles through which sharing one's journey may occur?

Do the congregation's leaders teach members the dynamics and disciplines of the spiritual life? Introductory, as well as more advanced teaching and experiential spiritual formation opportunities should be available at regular intervals. The program should be available for new and prospective members, as well as persons from across the community.

Does the congregation create, develop and support opportunities for members' spiritual renewal? How many retreats, prayer groups, covenant groups and renewal meetings exist or are held at your church? Are members encouraged to participate in local, regional and national spiritual renewal opportunities?

Does the congregation publicly witness to its spirituality? What occurrences and occasions are there for giving public witness to spirituality? How often do they occur? Is it considered acceptable in the church's culture to witness to one's spirituality?

Is personal witnessing occurring? Is personal witnessing employed for evangelism? Is witnessing made a part of sharing among members of the congregation? Is training given for witnessing? How many members participate in this training? How often is the training offered?

➡ IMPLEMENTATION IDEAS   Three implementation activities are appropriate for developing spirituality within a congregation. These activities include modeling by the leaders, teaching and supporting the members.

Modeling by the church leaders usually starts with the clergy. Sermons on spirituality and its practice are very desirable. Disclosure from the leaders of how they practice spirituality is very important. Lay leaders and other key laity should give witness to their spirituality. A description of one's spiritual journey and practices is important. Obviously, there will be opportunities for affirming that one is practicing spirituality; this kind of witness can be a powerful motivater for the one giving witness and for those who hear or see the witness. For example, that a leader is spending the weekend with a covenant group would set a good example.

Teaching persons the spiritual disciplines and how to live them in real life is crucial. A steady available diet of books on spirituality is a fine source of information. Classes, workshops and retreats focused on spirituality should be offered. Members should be encouraged to attend other activities, such as the Spiritual Formation Academy run by the Upper Room, the Curcillo retreats offered by the Catholic Church, or the Walk to Emmaus offered by The United Methodist Church. Teaching should include spiritual practices. One goal of teaching is to motivate and support persons as they begin and give themselves to spiritual formation.

Encouraging persons to form covenant groups, accountable discipleship groups, and so on will help them to get started. Individuals and groups need support and, at times, reinvigoration. The church leaders should regularly check with members to see how their spiritual practices are progressing. A careful, balanced and sensitive approach is needed. Some regular follow-up meetings can also be very useful.

➡ RESOURCE MATERIALS   Carretto, Carlo. *In Search of the Beyond.* Mary-
                              knoll, N.Y.: Orbis, 1976.
                              Harper, Steve. *Devotional Life in the Wesleyan*
Tradition. Nashville: The Upper Room, 1983.
Job, Rueben. *A Guide to Retreat for All God's Shepherds.* Nashville: Abingdon
    Press, 1994.
Job, Rueben, and Norman Shawchuck. *A Guide to Prayer for All God's People.*
    Nashville: The Upper Room, 1990.
————. *A Guide to Prayer for Ministers and Other Servants.* Nashville: The
    Upper Room, 1983.
Lewis, C. S. *Mere Christianity.* New York: Macmillan, 1986.
Nemeck, Francis, and Marie Teresa Coombs. *The Spiritual Journey.* Collegeville,
    Minn.: Liturgical Press, 1986.
Watson, David Lowes. *Accountable Discipleship.* Nashville: Discipleship
    Resources, 1985.
Willard, Dallas. *The Spirit of the Disciplines.* San Francisco: HarperCollins, 1988.

➡ RELIGIOUS QUALITIES

    ➡ SPIRITUALITY
    ➡ **BELIEVING**

➡ DEFINITION   A high-quality congregation has a clearly articulated, understood and communicated set of
beliefs. Doctrine is one of the defining elements of a church. A congregation's character is molded by its beliefs. But having a dogma is
not enough. Doctrine without faith is a deadly thing. A high-quality
congregation possesses both faith and dogma—so that both the clergy and the laity live out those beliefs as a central part of their lives.

This, then, is the second essential element of believing—having a
lively faith in the living Christ. A vital faith is very different from a
theological belief system or the doctrine to which a people may sub-
scribe. Put another way, a high-quality congregation believes with its
head—and with its heart.

➡ EXAMPLES   Virtually every study to understand what moti-
vates people when choosing a church home con-

cludes that theology or belief systems are not a prime consideration.

In recent decades The United Methodist Church, or private parties within it, have attempted to define the theology of the denomination. All such studies have concluded that the denomination has
no defining theology or doctrine. Also, over the past decades (since
the 1950s) The United Methodist Church has declined on almost
every scale normally used to measure the vitality of a denomination. On the other hand, however, studies into the characteristics of
large and growing churches consistently find that the senior pastor
is theologically more conservative than the laity, and that the leaders consistently hold forth a belief system as the norm for the congregation.

Putting all such considerations together seems to indicate that a
well-constructed belief system is important, but, alone, is not
enough to bring vitality to a denomination or a congregation. Other
qualities are needed. However, once a person does become active in
a church he or she does want to know what the church believes, and
doesn't want an incoherent doctrine as a basis for living.

Willow Creek Community Church in Barrington, Illinois, is perhaps the largest and most-studied Protestant church in America.
A defining characteristic of the church is the importance that the
leaders put upon the doctrine of the church. The weekend services
are targeted to the unchurched, while the Wednesday and Thursday
evening services are targeted to the members. To become a member
one must participate in an intensive new-member class. There the
new members are taught the doctrine and program of the church.
In addition, the doctrine of the church is consistently taught in the
Wednesday and Thursday services. These services are teaching
events. The members come with Bibles and notebooks, expecting to
be taught.

In addition to this, the senior pastor preaches an annual sermon
series (the same sermons) on the doctrine of the church. Thus the
members are consistently reminded of the church's doctrine, and
are regularly (once per year) taught the doctrines in a comprehensive manner.

In conversation with the members we find that they know their
particular doctrines and are striving to use them as the norm for

Christian living. Their doctrine is one form of glue that holds them together.

➡ DIAGNOSTIC QUESTIONS **Is there a publicly held and understood set of beliefs?** When and how are they made available to the members and other interested persons? Where are the doctrine and beliefs written? Who has copies?

Are there opportunities to clarify and deepen beliefs? How many sermons, workshops, retreats and classes are available to teach and deepen beliefs? How many persons attend workshops, retreats and classes intended to teach and deepen beliefs? Count them.

- Are new and potential members taught the beliefs?
- When and how are new and potential members taught beliefs?
- How often are beliefs presented or studied or discussed?
- Are beliefs shared with nonmembers?
- Is there a witness training program? Who and how many attend? How often and to whom do members witness?

➡ IMPLEMENTATION IDEAS Most organized religious groups have a set of beliefs, and these beliefs should be taught to the people regularly and consistently. In addition, with full support for diversity and an awareness of multicultural realities, the congregation should compose its own contextual set of beliefs or faith statements. These benchmark standards should regularly be taught and distributed to members and other interested parties.

A series of sermons, lectures, seminars and classes on the doctrine and standards of the congregation should be presented to all the people at least once each year. Judicatory personnel or seminary faculty might be invited to assist in the process. The beliefs should be clearly articulated, so that all members of the congregation know them and are equipped to present them in an inviting and compelling manner.

Another way to teach beliefs is to require that all new members participate in an educational experience so they know the local and denominational beliefs before joining. This is, however, never enough. It is important to rehearse the faith and doctrine of the church again and again.

One aspect of believing is sharing one's faith with others. Witnessing classes may be helpful in preparing members to share their beliefs with unchurched persons.

➡ RESOURCE MATERIALS   Note that each congregation, especially when defined by a denominational affiliation, will obviously turn to its own doctrinal heritage when communicating and witnessing benchmark beliefs. Many pastors shy away from communicating beliefs because often there is lack of agreement as to what constitutes correct belief, and thus the subject is ripe for controversy. If such timidity infects your congregation, one particular resource by

> One model of a witnessing class has the following elements:
> Participants first witness to each other. They then discuss each other's story. A shortened and clarified version is developed by each participant. The participants then role play witnessing with each other, using a specific and probable type of situation and context. Role plays are carried out and critiqued.

W. Paul Jones, *Theological Worlds* (Nashville: Abingdon Press, 1988), may be particularly effective. This book helps disparate parties come to terms with their diverse beliefs. Here are a few samples for congregations in either Wesleyan or Calvinist circles. Make a list of what you would use in setting forth this benchmark quality.

Calvin, John. *The Deity of Christ and Other Sermons.* Translated by Leroy Nixon. Grand Rapids: Eerdmanns, 1950.
Harper, Steve. *God's Call to Excellence.* Bristol House, 1989.
———. *John Wesley's Message for Today.* Francis Asbury Press, 1983.
Wesley, John. *The Works of John Wesley.* 19 vols. Edited by Albert Outler. Nashville: Abingdon Press, 1984.
Paul W. Chilcote, Wesley Speaks on Christian Vocation, Discipleship Resources, 1987.

> ➡ RELIGIOUS QUALITIES
>
> > ➡ SPIRITUALITY
> > ➡ BELIEVING
> > ➡ **VISION LED**

➡ DEFINITION Vision is God's dream of how things might be, dreamed within the heart of the person or congregation that faithfully works in harmony with God. As such the vision is God's first and ours second—a waking dream, dreamed within God's servant or God's people. Therefore, it is never quite proper to say, "I have a vision." It is more correct to say, "God's vision (for my ministry, for the congregation, and so on) has me." Vision grows out of the spirituality of individuals and the congregation together.

Stories in Scripture that describe vision generally follow a three-part theme. First, the vision gives the in-visioned one a new and clearer insight into who God is—*God's greatness*. Second, the vision gives the person or group a new and clearer insight into who she/he/they are—*my/our littleness, sinfulness, inability*. Third, the vision points toward new and exciting possibilities (now that I/we know who God is, and who I am/we are) for making the dream come true—*my/our mission*.

➡ EXAMPLES Examples of visions abound in the Scriptures. Consider Isaiah's vision (Isaiah 6). This vision story, and many like it in Scripture, contains the three thematic elements of vision:

Isaiah gains new insight into who God is

I saw the Lord sitting on a throne, high and lofty; and the hem of his robe filled the temple. Seraphs were in attendance above him; each had six wings: with two they covered their faces, and with two they covered their feet, and with two they flew. And one called to another and said: "Holy, holy, holy is the LORD of hosts; the whole earth is full of his glory." The pivots on the thresholds shook at the voices of those who called, and the house filled with smoke. (Isa. 6:1-4)

Isaiah gains new insight into who he is

And I said: "Woe is me! I am lost, for I am a man of unclean lips, and I live among a people of unclean lips; yet my eyes have seen the King, the LORD of hosts!"

Then one of the seraphs flew to me, holding a live coal that had been taken from the altar with a pair of tongs. The seraph touched my mouth with it and said: "Now that this has touched your lips, your guilt has departed and your sin is blotted out." (Isa. 6:5-7)

Isaiah gains new insight into new possibilities now that he knows who God is, and who he is

Then I heard the voice of the Lord saying, "Whom shall I send, and who will go for us?" And I said, "Here am I; send me!" And he said, "Go and say to this people. . . ." (Isa. 6:8-9)

The vision came from God and "captured" Isaiah quite unawares. Isaiah did not plan this vision; it came to him as a waking dream as he grieved and worried in the presence of God, in God's temple. Once taken by this vision, however, Isaiah was never the same; he gave his whole life to making it come true.

Vision did not pass away with the men and women whose stories are woven into the fabric of the Scriptures. Indeed, God still seeks to share God's dream with all who are willing and able to listen. God's dream is big enough to in-vision every person in the church. Indeed, while the congregation gives itself to its corporate vision, it is possible for every member to be energized and led by the dream God is dreaming in them—as individual persons before God.

The Open Door

Larry Dalton is a heating and air conditioning contractor and a member of First United Methodist Church, Michigan City, Indiana. Larry is the founder of The Open Door, a free clinic in Michigan City. The idea and vision were his. However he could never have done it alone. His devoted wife, Joyce, along with many others joined him to turn the vision into reality.

This great ministry was conceived, planned and has always been operated by lay persons, several of them members of the First United Methodist Church, Michigan City, Indiana. Others are members of Catholic, Salvation Army, Community churches and the local Jewish synagogue.

The idea of the clinic dawned upon Larry in 1987 through the sad experience of a woman who died without means of family to care for her. For a short while before her death she attended the First United Methodist Church in Michigan City where Larry and Joyce are members. She was very ill, but had long delayed seeing a doctor because she had only enough money for shelter and food. A few weeks after joining the congregation it was discovered that she had cancer, but it was too late. A few weeks later she died—at age forty.

The circumstances weighed heavily on Larry's mind and heart. He pondered the plight of many who must be ill, without money or family to care for them. Some weeks later in the midst of a most hectic day at his office, the vision of a free clinic for all who were ill and unable to purchase medical services burst, like a bolt of lightning, into his mind. So strong was the impulse that it startled him. He tried to put it away, but it demanded his attention. He *had* to do something! He felt that this was the Spirit of Christ stirring within him. This idea bothered him even more. To whom should he turn for help?

That same day Larry visited with the pastor. The pastor listened and then said, "Larry, I think this is an important moment for you and for us. I want you to tell your experience to the congregation next Sunday." The following Sunday Larry took the pastor's sermon time to share his experience with the congregation. He ended his story by saying, "If anyone understands what I am experiencing, will you please talk to me?"

Before Larry left the church building that day Dr. Amos Arney, a kind and saintly man, born in extreme poverty, who had in the face of every possible discouragement worked his way through medical school, and his wife, Juanita, an active member of the Salvation Army, cast their lots with Larry in the search for a way to help and heal the poor who were sick and unable to obtain medical attention. Others also offered their support that day.

By starting as a small group they met the next Sunday to dream and to plan. The Sunday meetings continued weekly for more than a year. Several others joined the weekly sessions. In the course of the year the group grew large and then declined and finally stabilized with some twelve or fourteen members. The Reverend John Wagner attended the meetings but he did not become active in the planning. His part was to encourage the group and to help them pray for discerning guidance.

Marilyn Wroblewski is a registered nurse and a social worker. She is a member of the Catholic Church. For some years she lived in Chicago, where she had volunteered at a free clinic. Upon moving to Michigan City she had attempted to start a free clinic but social service agencies, city officials and others never gave her a hearing. Marilyn heard of the Sunday meetings. She joined the group, and ultimately became the full time director of The Open Door.

The group identified the major obstacles they would need to remove along the way to opening a free clinic in Michigan City: the need for malpractice insurance, the need for volunteer doctors and nurses, the need for a place to house the clinic, the need for equipment and furnishings, drugs and medical supplies and the need for specialized services, such as laboratory tests, X-rays, etc.

All of these problems did exist, some of them proving to be seemingly insurmountable. But as each problem claimed its right to frustrate the group's effort by faith Larry Dalton and his group persevered.

The place for a clinic was provided.

To the credit of the health care institutions in Michigan City, national drug companies, and other suppliers, every one of whom Larry and others asked something gave generously. No one turned them away.

Thus in two years from the time the group first met together all things were provided for the clinic—save one: malpractice insurance. Indiana does not have a "Good Samaritan Law" to protect medical professionals who volunteer their services to charitable organizations. In Indiana volunteer professionals are not exempt from liability. The clinic would simply have to provide malpractice insurance or no professionals would volunteer.

After all other preparations for the clinic had been completed, the insurance agent called Larry. "Mr. Dalton," he said, "we have found a way to provide you the malpractice insurance for the cost of writing the policy." "How much is that?" Larry asked. "One thousand dollars a year," was the reply. The agency was able to do this because they discovered that by working within an obscure Indiana statute they could write a policy that was totally acceptable to the volunteer professionals and all other parties concerned.

The Open Door greeted its first patient on Feb. 27, 1989, two years after the vision was born in Larry Dalton's heart—as he pondered the death of a young woman who died without medical care. The first patient to enter the door was a man who complained of stomach pains. The attending volunteer physician discovered the man was in a condition of severe internal hemorrhaging. Without emergency care the man would have died that night. And so The Open Door began its life saving mission.

We cannot take the space to tell the whole story, but we do share the conviction of Larry Dalton that this kind of ministry is inspired and driven by a spiritual vision:

"I learned that if ever you feel you have an idea from the Holy Spirit, act on it—because the Holy Spirit will see you through.

"When this idea came to me I was overwhelmed. I kept asking, 'Why me? God, why are you bugging me?'

"The crucial step in this whole thing was when the pastor asked me to share my experience with the entire congregation immediately. I think if he would have given me much time to think about it I would never have done it, and the program may never have started.

"The vision was very clear but I could not understand why God would give it to me. I was not what most people would call a good Christian. I prayed a lot in those early days, 'Lord, take me as I am. I love you and I'll try to do better—but I probably won't make it.'"

The Open Door is now six years old. Here are some of its vital signs:

All services are provided by volunteers who donate their time (total of 3,506 hours in 1993) and expertise. Nineteen physicians, 80 nurses, 7 pharmacists, 3 registered dieticians, 6 social workers and over 200 lay members provide direct services to patients. Paid staff members include a full-time director, a full-time coordinator, and a part-time receptionist.

Twenty percent of the clinic's funding is provided by the Michigan City United Way. Additional funding comes from donations by private individuals and service organizations and churches.

In 1993, the clinic provided over 3,714 patients visits, 5,509 prescriptions were filled, and 790 patients were referred for lab work and X-rays. Additionally, 182 referrals were made to specialists in the community. Total operating expenses for 1993 were $105,364.00, not including the volunteer services and facilities.

The vision story of Larry Dalton serves to remind us that Isaiah's God is still able to dream God's dream in the hearts and efforts of those who dare to incarnate the vision God gives them. This is what the quality of being *vision led* is all about. And it doesn't take a theological degree to become a candidate for vision. Just as God shared God's vision with Isaiah many centuries ago, so also God is still sharing God's vision with laypersons. God gave the vision first to Larry, but vision is contagious. Many other people committed themselves to the vision as their own, and their efforts turned the vision into reality.

➡ COMMENTS   Vision can and should be happening at several levels in the congregation simultaneously. For example, the pastor is living out of a vision for his or her ministry that is conferred through the call to ministry. The leaders of the church may be leading out of a vision God has given them for the future of the church. The Sunday school superintendent may be ministering out of a vision God has given him or her for the Sunday school program. Individual members may have a vision for the church, and their respective roles in it. And of paramount importance, a corporate vision should infect the entire congregation for its ministry and its future.

A high-quality church will invite out and pay serious attention to all of these visions—the dreams God is dreaming in the congregation—all of the time.

The vision stories in the Scriptures also allude to some amazing examples of this quality.

Apparently God chooses not to share God's vision with lazy or "let's play it safe" people. God shares God's vision with people who are already doing something—even if it's the wrong thing. How unlikely that God would dream God's dream for the salvation of the Gentiles through Saul, who was actively engaged in the destruction of the church (Acts 9:1-16); or through Gideon, who was threshing wheat in a wine-press, because he was so afraid of the powerful Midianites (Judg. 6:11, 15).

Vision changes one's priorities and aligns one's thinking, feeling and doing into one coordinated thrust in which succeeding is no longer the issue. Giving oneself to the vision is the issue, against all odds, win or lose; for vision compels one to give one's self to the dream. So Gideon went against the powerful enemy with only 300 untrained soldiers, equipped only with a few candles, empty pitchers and trumpets (Judg. 7:16).

Vision inspires a contagious commitment. Apparently people would rather follow a person with a God-given dream than spend their time playing around in the wading pool. So the 300 ill-equipped soldiers followed Gideon, against all odds, just as the Israelite slaves followed Moses, against all odds.

This discussion of vision serves to show the interrelatedness and interdependency of the five religious qualities. When any one of the benchmark religious qualities is lacking, many of the others will be crippled. Vision has a mystical quality about it that can only be born out of the spirituality of the individual members and of the congregation as a whole. Mission is the incarnation of vision, the congregation's first-level attempt to make its dream real and visible. Only a people who believe firmly in God and in the church will ever open themselves up to the dream God desires to dream through them. We might diagram the interrelatedness of the religious qualities as follows:

Figure 2

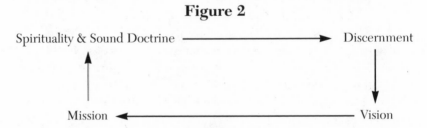

Most churches have some type of belief statement or creed. Many of the congregationally governed churches have a constitution and bylaws. Belief statements and governance documents, however, are not vision or mission statements. These documents are concerned with maintenance. Although they may have some utility for addressing problems, they do not motivate and point to innovation and/or change. Discernment, nurture of vision and mission clarification are processes which point toward new and fruitful directions for ministry and motivate people to volunteer their energies and resources to carry out the ministries.

Vision is a matter of perspective. When Moses sent the twelve spies to conduct a reconnaissance of the land beyond the Jordan, ten of them, from their perspective, saw the inhabitants as unconquerable giants against whom the weak and puny Israelites could never prevail: "And to ourselves we seemed like grasshoppers" (Num. 13:33). They had one perspective. But two of the spies saw a totally different reality: "The land . . . is an exceedingly good land. If the LORD is pleased with us, he will bring us into this land and give it to us" (Num. 14:7-8). They had caught Moses' vision of a promised land. They saw a different reality.

➡ DIAGNOSTIC QUESTIONS   A congregation may diagnose to what extent their vision is a benchmark in the life of the church with the following questions:

Does the congregation have a vision for its future? Does the congregation know where it wants to be ten years from now? How will the community be different because the church is there?

Is there a vision statement for the church? Is the vision statement in written form? Is the vision statement widely distributed and clearly understood by the members of the congregation?

Is the vision statement used? When is the vision statement used? How is it used? How often is it used?

Do the pastor and key lay leaders hold forth a vision for the church? Is the vision of the leaders believable? Inspiring?

Do the leaders invite and support expressions of vision from all persons and areas of ministry? Does the pastor preach and teach about vision? Are there classes in discernment to teach about vision and prayerful listening for God's leading?

➡ IMPLEMENTATION IDEAS   One significant way to develop a corporate vision is to use a discernment process. Discernment will be discussed in some detail later in this book.

Another way to foster vision is to install a small group or cell movement in the church, the purpose of which is to allow persons to support one another in a corporate living out of the spiritual disciplines. The pastor and leaders create an expectancy within these groups that God will sooner or later lead them into a vision of ministry they can perform as a group. Some of the finest ministries the church has ever launched will come from such spiritual life groups who expect that the fruits of their experience will be lived out in ministry to the world.[2]

➡ RESOURCE MATERIALS   Adams, John. *Transforming Leadership Vision to Results*. Niles River Press, 1986.

Bennis, Warren, and Burt Nanus. *Leaders: The Strategies for Taking Charge*. New York: Harper & Row, 1985.

Nanus, Burt. *Visionary Leadership*. San Francisco: Jossey-Bass Publishers, 1992.

Phillips, Donald T. *Lincoln on Leadership*. New York: Warner Books, 1992.

Shawchuck, Norman, and Roger Heuser. *Leading the Congregation*. Nashville: Abingdon Press, 1993.

➡ **RELIGIOUS QUALITIES**

➡ SPIRITUALITY
➡ BELIEVING
➡ VISION LED
➡ **MISSION DRIVEN**

➡ DEFINITION   A mission establishes ministry directions and evaluative standards for turning the vision into reality. A vision is more mystical; the mission is more systematic and therefore based in planning. Mission is the group's first-level attempt to incarnate its vision—to make its vision visible. Mission is the person's or group's response to the vision that God has given; it establishes the "what" and the "why" of ministry.

It is generally useful to express mission in a succinct statement—that is, in a *mission statement*. A mission statement gives direction for making our vision come true. A mission statement puts flesh and

42

blood on the vision. If you will, it incarnates the vision, so that everyone can see the vision as it is brought into reality.

➡ EXAMPLES Virtually all of the vision stories (some might say, *call narratives*) in Scripture conclude with the in-visioned one coming to a clear sense of mission.

From the time we are first introduced to Moses (Exod. 2:11-15; 3:10), we see that his mission was to liberate the Israelite slaves from Egyptian oppression. At first he tried to do so through power and violence—and failed. Then, forty years later he was envisioned through an encounter with God and was reminded of his mission. Empowered by his vision and call he once again set out to accomplish his mission—using far different ways and means. But through it all, his mission remained unchanged.

The covenant group, referred to above, that launched a free clinic in Indiana took its mission from Matthew 25:36, "To care for those who are sick."

The development of mission is coherent with being *communicative,* having significant *lay participation and lay power,* respect for *community* and development of *high expectations.*

➡ COMMENTS We once had the opportunity to facilitate an ad hoc consultation committee formed by a small denomination. The purpose of the consultation was to help the denominational executives establish better relationships with the congregations. One of the topics discussed was the necessity of having a denominational mission statement that was owned by the clergy and lay members of the congregations.

One of the members of the consultation had recently retired as the manager of operations in Central and South America for a very large bank. He said that the bank discovered in order for their mission statement to have a real effect on the operations of the company, it has to be communicated to every employee of the organization *fifty-seven* times a year. He claimed that every manager must report regularly how he or she is communicating the mission to all of his or her employees, fifty-seven times during the year.

Then another person commented that a large discount retail corporation requires that every employee hear the company's mission at least *fifty* times a year. He said that unless the sales clerk is reminded of the store's mission at least fifty times a year, he or she will tend to forget it just when they need to remember it most—when they are dealing with a difficult or irate customer.

In his book, *Selling the Dream*, Guy Kawasaki lists three qualities of a mission:

- **Short.** Brief and simple mission statements are easy to understand and remember. Brevity and simplicity are also evidence of clear thinking. For example, the Girl Scouts' mission statement is: "To help a girl reach her highest potential." It's short, simple, easy to understand and remember.
- **Flexible.** Flexible mission statements last a long time. For example, "Ensuring an adequate supply of water," is inflexible and confining. It may not survive the next rainy season. The Macintosh Division mission statement was "to improve the creativity and productivity of people." It was flexible enough to accommodate development of computers and peripheral products such as laser printers, software, books and training aids for a long time.
- **Distinctive.** Distinctive mission statements differentiate your cause from other organizations with similar missions. The "Centre for Living with Dying" has a unique mission statement, "To provide emotional support for the dying and bereaved," that sets it apart from most other nonprofit and humanitarian organizations in Silicon Valley.[3]

Moses' mission, referred to above, can be stated in seven words: "To liberate the Israelites from Egypt's oppression." That's just about long enough to state one's mission. If the basic mission statement is more than twenty-five words people won't remember it; and if they can't remember it, they won't accomplish it.

➡ DIAGNOSTIC QUESTIONS **Does the congregation have a mission statement based on its vision?** Is the mission statement in written form? Where is the mission statement available?

Have members recently (in the last three or four years) created or reviewed the congregation's mission statement? Who participated in preparing the mission statement? The more the better. Who was involved in approving the mission statement? The broader the participation in approving the mission the better. The quality controlled by Lay Power is also being served by mission clarification.

Are members knowledgeable of the mission statement? The entire congregation or a representative sample should be surveyed to determine the extent of familiarity with the mission statement. Everyone should know it and support it.

Is the mission statement used as a gauge to test the congregation's decisions and activities? In which decision-making situations are the vision and/or mission statement used? What happens when there are interests competing with the vision and/or mission statement?

➡ IMPLEMENTATION IDEAS Developing a mission statement is a much more cognitive and rational process than dreaming a vision. A mission statement requires the following:

- The mission statement should derive from the vision statement.
- Goals expressed should have measurable criteria for success.
- Planning should include a time line for achieving goals.
- The development of a mission statement should be carried out with wide participation of all constituencies.

Several processes can be used to help determine the mission of the congregation. One process that has proven very popular over the past decade is described in *Management for Your Church*, by Alvin Lindgren and Norman Shawchuck.[4] Another simple and yet powerful approach will be presented in the discussion of *discerning*, in the next section. An example of a third process for mission clarification that can involve large numbers of persons is the Nominal Group Technique.[5]

A progressive panel is often used to develop vision and mission statements. One simply builds a hierarchy of groupings. The lowest-level groups develop the initial statements. These smallest groups combine

A mission statement development process might utilize the Nominal Group Technique (NGT), which employs focus groups. One could constitute focus groups for each part of the vision statement. Or one could constitute focus groups of workers and participants in each program area of the church. The results of the focus groups would then be compared and combined to discover the more comprehensive mission to which the congregation might devote itself.

Let us consider what each focus group will do. The group should first receive instruction as to the purpose of a mission statement. A specific format should be recommended. The group will be presented the portion of the vision statement on which they will focus. They will be asked to write down all the mission ideas that come to mind and formulate possible missions statements. The facilitator of the group will ask each member in turn to read one of the proposed mission statement. Members will be asked to hold any comments and discussion until all the statements are read; clarification questions, however, are allowed. Each successive speaker will be asked not to duplicate any previous statement. Once the lists of statements are exhausted, the first phase is completed. The director of the group will propose elimination and consolidation of any mission statements that duplicate or overlap each other.

The next step is to invite persons to present support for statements they like and opposition to statements to which they object.

When the discussion is over, the group ranks the statements. The top-ranked items will be presented to the focus groups as a whole. The process of consolidation may be continued across statements from the different groups. If desired, a ranking may be prepared across all the statements presented by all the groups.

with other groups to form the next larger groups. These groups then discuss and agree on a new statement. This procedure continues until there is only one group. For instance, we might start with eight groups. The eight groups form four. The four groups form two groups and the two groups eventually become one. This means that every individual is involved in four rounds of discussion in progressively larger groups.

Another way of developing statements is with a dialectical circle. The procedure consists of forming a small number of groups. Each group develops a first draft of the statement. Each draft is sent to the next group for revision. When all the groups have finished their drafts, they send it to the next group for revision. The process continues as each draft is revised by each group. When a draft returns to the originating group, the revisions are finished. Then a discussion is held to reach consensus on the preferred draft.

➡ **RESOURCE MATERIALS** Delbecq, Andre, et al. *Group Techniques for Program Planning: Nominal Group Techniques and Delphi Process.* Green Briar, Madison, WI.: 1986.

Lindgren, Alvin, and Norman Shawchuck. *Management for Your Church.* Leith, ND: Spiritual Growth Resources, 1977, pp 45-59.

➡ **RELIGIOUS QUALITIES**

> ➡ SPIRITUALITY
> ➡ BELIEVING
> ➡ VISION LED
> ➡ MISSION DRIVEN
> ➡ **DISCERNING**

➡ **DEFINITION** Discernment is a product of the spiritual life. Discernment is a decision-making process that seeks faithfully to involve God in the decision making. It is a process built upon silence and prayer, and a searching of the Scriptures to discover the missional directions and ministries toward which God may be leading the church. As such, discernment is both a group process and a way of life. It involves both the head and the heart. The *overarching* goal is to prepare persons to have a discerning heart—the ability to listen to God in all times and situations.

Christian discernment means living in such a way that we know beyond knowing that Jesus Christ actually does shape, color and govern all our decisions, both great and small.[6]

A discerning congregation develops and follows a corporate vision and has a missional statement based on it. Discernment is the process by which the group discovers its mission and the ministries that will accomplish the mission.

➡ **EXAMPLES** The Christian church has always claimed that it is possible to know the leading of God in our lives and ministries. This "coming to know" is called *discernment*, or *discerning the mind of God*. The ancient church fell back upon this faithful listening process whenever it seriously desired to know God's leading. For example, Acts 15 is an entire chapter dedicated to show-ing us the discernment process through which the early church sought to discern the mind of God regarding the conditions under which Gentile believers were to be welcomed into the church.

Two more modern church leaders who taught discernment as a means of knowing and responding to the will of God were St. Ignatius of Loyola and Joseph Cardinal Cardijn, Bishop of Belgium in the time of the two world wars.[7]

St. Ignatius of Loyola and the Jesuits. St. Ignatius of Loyola founded the Society of Jesus, often called the Jesuits. In the 1500s Ignatius codified discernment as it had developed from the time of the apostolic church, and then worked out a method to teach dis-cernment to the people who came to him for spiritual direction. He gathered this process together under the rubric of "The Spiritual Exercises," or "discerning the mind of God." Ignatius taught that discernment could be practiced by individuals and by communities.

In teaching discernment, Ignatius stressed the importance of using analytical research and prayer; bringing both head and heart to the decision-making process.[8]

Joseph Cardinal Cardijn. Joseph Cardijn firmly held to the idea that the priest or pastor could not tell laypersons what their ministry should be, since only God calls the laity to ministry. He said, howev-er, that the priest did have an important role—and that is to teach laypersons how to pray, how to meditate upon Scriptures and how to open their eyes to see the needs around them. He named the move-ment in this method: See, Judge, Act.[9] Cardijn's chief contribution to the subject of discernment is that he showed even children could be taught to discover their ministry.

- **See!** Open your eyes and look around you. What human needs do you see? Look, as if through the eyes of Jesus. Pray that God will open your eyes to see as God sees when God looks upon your community. Look as though you have never seen this community or these people before. Use whatever means you can to help you see and understand the needs around you. *What do you see?*

- **Judge!** Make critical judgments about what you see in the light of Scripture and the best of social literature. Is there that in Scripture which teaches that you should respond to such need? How are such needs responded to in Scripture? What is there in time-honored and contemporary social literature that teaches how you should respond to such need? What does this literature teach about human response to such needs? *What do the Scriptures teach?*
- **Act!** Whenever God has opened your eyes to a need, and you find the Scriptures (and literature) urging human response, you know God is calling you to do what you can. God never asks more than you can do. God asks only that you do what you can. When a community does what it can, however small, it unleashes faith and energy and, through Christ, is able to do what it cannot do alone. *Do what you can!*

A simple diagram of Cardinal Cardijn's discernment method might be as follows:

Figure 3

How to Know the Will of God for our Ministry

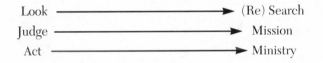

Look —————————————▶ (Re) Search
Judge —————————————▶ Mission
Act —————————————▶ Ministry

Terry Fullam and St. Paul's Episcopal Church, Darien Connecticut. Terry Fullam was appointed the rector of St. Paul's Episcopal Church in Darien, Connecticut in 1972. When he arrived he found a small congregation, not growing in any significant manner. His first meeting with the parish council would prove a landmark event in the life of the church and in Terry's ministry.

At that meeting, he made some comments about Jesus Christ being the Head of the Church and asked the members whether they thought this were so. The common reply was "Well, yes. I guess so." Then Terry asked a second question, which ultimately would serve to change everything about the way the congregation would make and carry out its corporate decisions: "If Jesus is the Head of *this* church, what is the function of the Head with the rest of the body?"

As the council members pondered the question with their new rector, they stumbled upon thinking about the church as an organism rather than an organization, and they asked a question of their own: "If the congregation is a living body and Christ is its living Head, how should we go about doing our work as the parish council?"

The group decided that Christ would lead them as a body—together. There would be no private revelation to individuals. Rather, Christ would share Christ's revelation with all of them, as a single, unified body. The group and their new rector thereupon decided that they would no longer seek to make decisions with debate and vote. Instead, they would always look for a sense of agreement that might allow them to say, "We have been instructed by the Head of the Church."

For every important matter they would generate many ideas, yet be always willing to give them up. There would be no need to argue or to persuade one another, since they would all be seeking to find a collectivity, unity. And, they reasoned, when they had discovered the leading of Christ, the Head, there would be a corporate sense of peace, joy and harmony. With these decisions, the parish council members committed themselves to Christ and to one another in faith that Christ would lead them corporately.

In his very first sermon to the congregation, and for several sermons in succession, Terry hammered home the point that Jesus Christ is the head of the church, and that he is well able to run the church and to make its decisions.

"But," many asked, "how is Christ able to make decisions in the congregation today?" This opened the door for Terry to teach the congregation about *discernment,* listening in to the directions God has for us. In due time, the congregation as a body committed itself (as the parish council before them) to making no important decisions until the members were confident they were being led by Christ, the Head of the congregation.

This commitment on the part of the rector, the parish council and the congregation became the *modus operandi* in conducting the church's affairs for the seventeen years that Terry served as its rector. Along the way, St. Paul's Church became one of the fastest growing Episcopal churches in the United States.

In preparing this story we interviewed Terry to be certain our description was correct. In the course of the interview, he said, "All of the results we achieved were due to the fact that we found out the Lord was able to lead us collectively. So we became a church without factions or conflict. The congregation experienced an astonishing sense of unity. We learned that unity is a gift from God, not the goal. The goal is to discern the mind of the Lord. When a congregation commits itself to this, unity will be given to it."[10]

➡ COMMENTS   Broadly defined, discernment is listening to God. There are many methods of discernment. The earliest record of the ancient church attempting to discern the mind of God regarding important matters is found in Acts 1:23-26, to fill the vacancy left by the resignation of Judas from the company of the twelve apostles. Discernment was again used when the first deacons were selected (Acts 6:3-7).

And it is seen as a fully developed decision-making process in Acts 15, as the church faced the most crucial decision it has ever faced: deciding the means by which the Gentile people would be welcomed into Christianity. The church followed a process by which they were finally able to say, "It seems good to us—and to the Holy Spirit." Discernment is a faithful decision-making process by which the church does not decide until the people have come to peace about the decision, and they have a witness of God's participation that allows them to say with humility and authenticity, "This decision seems good to us and to the Holy Spirit."

Discernment is not following *Robert's Rules of Order* to achieve a democratic vote. These methods introduce debate and contest, and finally result in making some people winners and others losers. No one likes to lose. Discernment makes everyone winners. After twenty years of working with troubled and conflicted congregations, we are convinced that a primary cause of division and infighting lies in the use of *Robert's Rules of Order,* and the vote as the major means of deciding the future and choosing the ministries of the church. A congregation will never reach its highest quality potential until it dispenses with decision-making processes that pit one person or group against another in a contest of verbal abilities and power maneuvers. Discernment is indeed an essential ingredient in building a high-quality church. It generates energy for ministry and fosters community.

➡ DIAGNOSTIC QUESTIONS **Do the leaders and decision makers in the congregation sincerely believe that God hears and answers prayer?** When making serious decisions or seeking to resolve differences do they take prayer as seriously as their conversation with each other? Do they believe that God is able to actively enter and influence the decisions?

Do the leaders have an established method for discerning the Mind of God? Have they been trained in the method? Are new members of decision-making bodies trained in discernment at the time they come into the group? Do they have an understanding of the type of decision that will be voted on, and which will be given over to discerment?

Do the pastors and teachers preach and teach discernment to the laity? Are the people of the church urged to practice discernment for their personal, family and business decisions? Do the leaders and teachers conduct seminars and classes in discernment for individual, family and group decisions?

➡ IMPLEMENTATION IDEAS The ultimate goal is to have a discerning heart; to be ever sensitive to the still, small voice of God offering guidance and wisdom in the everyday affairs as well as the monumental decisions we must make.

There are many decisions that are of such little consequence that a simple vote will do. However, when the decision is of crucial importance, or there is serious disagreement over alternatives, then discernment should be used. Even more important than this is to consistently teach and preach that discernment is a way of life.

Classes and seminars on discernment may be conducted in which a variety of discernment methods are presented, and persons are allowed to practice them. Spiritual life retreats offer much opportunity for the participants to "discern," to listen to God. A three-month class might present the general history and content of discernment in one or two sessions and then move on to feature a particular discernment method in each session.

Personal discernment is especially important around nodal events and transitions; i.e., graduation, marriage, a serious illness, a death, an unexpected large financial gain, etc. The sensitive pastor will find many opportunities to lead persons into a season of discernment.

➡ **RESOURCE MATERIALS**   Cardijn, Joseph Cardinal. *Laymen into Action.* London: Geoffrey Chapman, 1964. Although this book is out of print, it can still be found in seminary libraries and is well worth the search. This book is perhaps the best theology of lay ministry ever written.

Foster, Richard. *Celebration of Discipline.* 10th ed. San Francisco: Harper & Row, 1992. This book contains a brief survey of discernment and discernment processes; it is a very good review of the subject.

Ignatius of Loyola. *The Spiritual Exercises of St. Ignatius Loyola.* Translated by Elisabeth Meier Tetlow. Lanham, Md.: University Press of America, 1987.

Morris, Danny. *Yearning to Know God's Yearning.* Nashville: The Upper Room, 1992.

Schlosser, Robert. *Miracle in Darien.* Logos International, 1979.

Sheeran, Michael J. *Beyond Majority Rule: Voteless Decisions in the Religious Society of Friends, Philadelphia Yearly Meeting of the Religious Society of Friends.* Philadelphia, 1983.

The religious qualities combine to afford persons a high-quality religious experience. Without a high-quality religious experience, there is little grounding for the remainder of the qualities that we will explain. We do not pretend that the five qualities discussed above exhaust the list of what might contribute to a high-quality religious experience. You may wish to add another quality, or more, in the quest for building quality into your congregation.

The benchmark quality of religious experience is, furthermore, certainly not restricted to the paid professionals in the church. So now we proceed to a consideration of the lay-led qualities. We intentionally place these qualities second in our list. Intentionally, because we believe that the participation and power of the laity is indispensable to all efforts to build a high-quality church. The pastor and leaders have a crucial role to play in achieving quality, but without the participation of the laity and a continuous expansion of lay power, the church has no chance of realizing its potential for quality.

2 - Lay-Led Qualities

LAY-LED QUALITIES ARE THE MEANS BY WHICH A CONGREGATION EVER EXPANDS ITS MINISTRY BASE, FOR LAY PARTICIPATION IS A FUNDAMENTAL KEY TO ACHIEVING QUALITY.

➡ SIGNIFICANT LAY PARTICIPATION
➡ GUIDED BY LAY POWER

L ay-Led Qualities are the means by which a congregation ever expands its ministry base, for lay participation is a fundamental key to achieving quality. Without a broad and ever expanding base of lay leadership and participation at every level of the church organization and ministry, the church will never approach its potential for quality. The laity comprises by far the greatest number of people in a congregation. Their serious and enthusiastic participation is necessary to succeed in achieving all of the qualities. The church's greatest gift comes from having committed and active laity with power to serve.

➡ LAY-LED QUALITIES

➡ SIGNIFICANT LAY PARTICIPATION

➡ DEFINITION Laity are involved in leadership and contribute to most, if not all, activities of the church. The present generations of actual and potential churchgoers eschew top-down bureaucracies. They expect to be full participants in directing the affairs that affect them and the organizations to which they belong. Without this, they will never be serious and committed members.

➡ EXAMPLES **Lay Ministers Serve as Spiritual Directors and Retreat Leaders.** Earlier we discussed a congregation in Ohio that decided to become a place where people can come for spiritual development. One outstanding feature of this ministry is that it is carried out by seventy-five laypersons who are trained to serve as spiritual directors and retreat leaders. Things "spiritual" are too often felt to be in the domain of the ordained minister. This congregation, however, is proving there is perhaps no ministry that trained and equipped lay ministers cannot fulfill with distinction. Whatever exceptions there are to this are more matters of attitude and aging denominational polities than they are matters of fact.

Colonial Hills United Methodist Church, San Antonio, Texas. Bill Easum served as senior of Colonial Hills United Methodist Church for twenty-four years. When he arrived, the congregation numbered less than fifty in worship. When he left in 1993, worship attendance averaged nearly 1,000.

Shortly after Bill's coming, the congregation established the vision statement that "Every member is a minister." Staff members were not expected to do ministry, but to equip the laity to be lay ministers to one another and to the unchurched. Ordained clergy were referred to as "equipping pastors" and laity as "lay ministers." As the church grew, the program and pastoral staff equaled one person for every 100 people in worship, so that this equipping could take place. By the time Bill left Colonial Hills, the program and pastoral staff had been reduced below the one-to-one hundred ratio due to the number of small-group ministries and the quality of equipped lay ministers. The church functions with only two salaried secretaries, including the financial secretary.

Saddleback Valley Community Church, Lake Forest, California. Rick Warren established the Saddleback Valley Community Church in 1980, upon graduation from seminary. Beginning with just one family, the church grew to 8,000 in attendance by 1993. In addition, the church has sponsored twenty-four offspring congregations in the southern California area.

One of the key components of Saddleback's philosophy of ministry is the mobilization of every member into ministry. Over 1,000 lay ministers lead and direct the various ministries of the church.

➡ COMMENTS   We have interviewed each of the pastors and several key lay leaders of the churches discussed above. They all assert that the policy to have every member in active ministry is a fundamental key to their growth—ample proof that significant lay participation can go far to foster quality, with growth following as a consequence of doing things right.

Lay participation, however, is not enough to ensure quality. Each of these congregations also demonstrates virtually all of the qualities discussed in this book. True quality cannot be achieved by emphasizing only one benchmark quality. High quality requires the correct mix of the qualities that represent the best your congregation has to offer.

How very different is the practice of these three churches, in placing its members in ministry, from that of the great majority of churches in North America today. For most churches, the method still followed is the annual nominating committee process in which a small group cloisters itself in secret to determine the "right person for the right job." This process, as it is generally practiced, has at least two major flaws.

First, perhaps more than 90 percent of the jobs handled by nominating committees are administrative; the committees appoint persons to administer the administrative details of the church's programs—worship committee, finance committee, trustees, board members, Sunday school committee and so on. In this way, the church inadvertently sends the message that the most important thing is administration, not the work of ministry in the world.

Second, in most instances the majority of the persons who are nominated do not know why they were chosen as the person most qualified or desired for the job, and most do not know they have been nominated until the moment they hear their name read at the annual church meeting—if they happen to be in attendance.

Church leaders should be working at developing a congregation with significant lay participation. Being communicative and training congregation members are important steps in developing lay participation.

➡ DIAGNOSTIC QUESTIONS **Does the laity participate in presenting the worship services?** What roles do laypersons take? How many different persons participate? How often are they involved? How are they chosen? Why are they chosen? Who is chosen?

Does the laity participate in planning and leading the education programs? Who runs the Sunday school? Who runs the adult education program? Are the Sunday school materials purchased from a publishing house, or do laypersons have the motivation and guidance to participate in designing and writing the materials? Are laity perceived as incapable of creating their own teaching materials?

Does the laity participate in preparing and carrying out the other programs? Who decides, arranges, runs and evaluates the programs?

Does the laity participate in ministries outside the walls of the church? Who decides, arranges, runs and evaluates the ministries?

Does the laity participate in administering and managing the church? What functions do laypersons carry out? Are they personally recruited or elected? Is the laity heard and respected?

Is there a systematic way that members of the congregation are heard?

When in private, does the staff make fun of the congregation and members' ideas? Is there a pattern in the church of ridiculing or disparaging lay members for inferior knowledge, skills or motivation? What are the relative percentages of participation of clergy and laity, paid and volunteer staff members, new and old members?

➡ IMPLEMENTATION IDEAS Make lay participation a major commitment of your congregation. To do this, four actions are important: recruiting, respecting, training and recognition. If the full participation of the laity in planning and carrying out the programs of the church is not sincerely honored and vigorously advocated by the paid staff, laypersons will likely be reluctant to volunteer, and if they do volunteer, many will not give the job their best effort. So, beyond announcing a new policy for assuring and guiding lay participation, it is important to implement it at the top; the board and staff must take the lead. A committee or task force might be helpful in developing and managing the participation of laity.

Several steps are necessary for achieving high-quality lay participation: effective recruitment, job descriptions, support of high expectations (discussed later in this book) and training.

Recruitment

Make a list of potential workers. Find out their skills and interests. A school principal may be well qualified to function as a volunteer director of the religious education program. On the other hand, however, it may be the last thing the principal wants to do while "off the job." Any satisfactory lay recruitment process must be sensitive not only to the skills of the individual but also to his or her volunteer ministry interests.

Job Descriptions

Job descriptions are an important tool in recruitment (though laity are sometimes resistant to calling their ministry a "job," just as any paid or ordained religious professional would resist the secular implications). Some persons are concerned about their ability to measure up to the task; others may be concerned with making a commitment to a task they do not fully understand. In either case the job description is helpful.

When expanding lay participation, the pastor and key lay leaders should understand the attitude and behavioral differences between a *standing committee* and a *task force*. Standing committees tend to control, maintain and preserve; they generally are not interested in innovation, and they oppose change. Task forces, in contrast, are generally interested in creating something new or creating change in an existing program. As such, a task force is a vehicle for getting projects up and running. Some persons prefer to work on standing committees; others are bored silly on a standing committee and will always prefer an intense, time-bounded commitment, which is characteristic of a task force.

Training Lay Ministers

A ministry team must be provided for the volunteer workers before the leaders have the right to demand quality of anyone. It is unconscionable to demand high levels of commitment of persons and then not give them the resources, skills and support needed to meet the expectations of the leaders and congregation. Training also makes it easier to recruit persons who are willing to make the demanding effort necessary to do a high-quality job. People will more readily volunteer for tough jobs when they know they will be given the resources to succeed. *No one wants to fail.* It is the fear of failure that keeps good people from taking on tough jobs. For many, the prospect of training relieves their uncertainties regarding their ability to do the job well. Some people may find church training an important adjunct to assist them in their professional life.

Beyond providing for the spiritual formation of the members and workers of the congregation, the pastor's most important responsibility is to train the leadership teams to perform their specific ministries well.

Attention should be paid to two types of training: general skill training and specific training for a given ministry. Areas of general training that are important for all workers include communications, conflict management, budgeting, problem solving and so on. Specific training is targeted to the particular assignment a person is expected to fill, that is, teaching skills for teachers, computer skills for office workers and so on. For larger congregations, a system of apprentice training with a path toward authority and autonomy in each position is desirable. A pattern of three-year rotating chairs for ministry teams (to be discussed under the section "Has Many Programs") is one model that will bear much fruit.

Appropriate recognition programs (also to be discussed in "Has Many Programs") serve well to support lay participation.

➡ RESOURCE MATERIALS Cardijn, Joseph Cardinal. *Laymen into Action.* London: Geoffrey Chapman, 1964 (available only in libraries).

Easum, Bill. *The Church Growth Handbook.* Nashville: Abingdon Press, 1988. Chapter 3, Lay Participation.

Palmer, John. *Equipping for Ministry.* Gospel Publications, 1985.

➡ Lᴀʏ-Lᴇᴅ Qᴜᴀʟɪᴛɪᴇs

➡ Sɪɢɴɪꜰɪᴄᴀɴᴛ Lᴀʏ ᴘᴀʀᴛɪᴄɪᴘᴀᴛɪᴏɴ
➡ **Gᴜɪᴅᴇᴅ ʙʏ Lᴀʏ Pᴏᴡᴇʀ**

➡ Dᴇꜰɪɴɪᴛɪᴏɴ   In a church guided by lay power, the direction and control of church matters are heavily influenced or guided by the congregation. Policy and methods are developed to facilitate the expansion of lay participation at a stipulated but incremental annual rate—perhaps 5 percent more participation each year. (No congregation can achieve huge and lasting gains in one year.) Both breadth and depth of lay participation are expanding.

Discussion of the use of lay power in determining and carrying out the directions and ministries of the church is fraught with difficulties. Thorough attention to this quality could fill an entire book. We do not, however, wish to give the impression that the laity should rule to the exclusion of the important role of the ordained leadership in guiding the congregation. We do not anticipate an all-powerful laity and a slavish clergy. Rather, we support a blending or leveling of the two sources of power: the clergy power and the congregation's power.

However, this quality in a congregation suggests that eventually laypersons (all of them) are heard and their opinions honored. Furthermore, the laity will assume major roles in policy making, and in planning and carrying out the ministries of the church.

We will now proceed to consider some examples.

➡ Exᴀᴍᴘʟᴇs   **The Laity Influences the Church Board.**
Lyle Schaller (in his seminars) has observed that over many centuries the single most divisive issue in the church has been its music. Wars have been waged over this issue. At scores of congregations where we consult, we have observed serious conflict regarding the music program. One church in particular undertook to resolve this conflict by being guided by lay power.

Grumbling and complaints about the church music program had

been heard for years. A member brought an informal complaint to the church board chairperson, stating that a number of people were requesting that the board take action on this matter. The board chairperson replied he was aware of the complaints, and that the pastor had spoken to the music director (who had served in this position for thirty years) about the complaints. The music director, however, said he knew what good church music was, and that those who were complaining should get used to it.

Several months later a group of members appeared at the church board meeting and presented a petition calling for a greater variety of styles and types of music, including instrumental music and vocal ensembles. The petition bore the signatures of fifty people, one-fourth of the Sunday service attendance.

After much discussion the board decided that a petition of fifty loyal participants in the worship services was not to be taken lightly. Whatever was going on, they could no longer ignore it. The board decided to appoint three focus groups comprising persons who were faithful in worship attendance and some who had recently stopped attending. One group would be directed by the music committee, one by the petition group, and one by the board. A congregational meeting would then be called to vote on the proposals developed out of the information generated from the focus groups. (This approach will be described again when we discuss the benchmark quality of pastoral care.)

The focus groups were conducted and the results were presented to the congregation. The focus groups clearly showed that for the services to remain relevant to the people that it could reach, the music program would need to be greatly expanded and diversified to include the types of music that would be appealing and relevant to all of the congregation.

A Building Committee Learns a Lesson in Being Guided by Lay Power. A pastor whom we interviewed provided us with this second example of being guided by lay power.

"I learned my lesson about inside-out thinking at the church I served before coming to St. John's.[1] We conducted a large renovation project of the church buildings. We appointed a building committee of highly competent persons: engineers, architects, contractors and, of course, the president of the women's group. As it turned out, all of these persons were over forty years old. Everything went along without a hitch until we began making plans for the renovation of the infants' and toddlers' nurseries. Suddenly the mothers of the small children began complaining about everything we were planning to do.

"We called a meeting of the building committee and several young couples who had children in our nursery programs. It was not a quiet meeting. The members of the building committee were trying to explain and defend their plans for the nurseries, but the young mothers would not be put off. Finally, one of the young mothers exploded, 'You old fuddy-duddies will never know how to design a nursery until you look at it from twenty-four inches off the floor!'

"I pondered her remarks for several days, wondering what to make of her comment. I finally admitted she wasn't being funny or cruel. She literally sensed that we would never know how to design a nursery until we got out of our forty- and fifty-year-old skins and looked at the nursery through the eyes and experience of a little child; someone standing about two feet high.

"We expanded the building committee to include several of the young parents and we designed the nurseries looking through the eyes of the young mothers, for their eyes were a lot closer to the experience of the little children than were ours."

The inclusion of the young parents in designing the nursery facilities allowed the building committee to be guided by lay power—in this instance the young parents who would use the nurseries after they were in operation. This example of outside-in thinking is often required for the benchmark of lay power.[2]

➡ COMMENTS There is much talk today, especially in seminaries, about empowering the laity. A fine slogan, but still we must ask, "Empowered for what?" Lay power already exists. Except in very large churches every member acts as though he or she is a member of the board of directors. They all have opinions, and many express their opinions quite freely.

Every layperson is free to exercise his/her power in most decisive ways—the power of the purse, and the power of the empty pew;

they can stop giving and they can stop attending. Beyond this, in many Protestant churches the laity can vote a pastor in or out, can reverse virtually any decision reached by the board, and can stall important decisions indefinitely. This is power!

Power misguided, however, is very destructive. To build a church of high quality is to require that the policies and ministries are guided by lay power. This requires that the laity is taught and supported to use its power wisely, always for the building up of the church; to edify, and never to tear it down. Because power may go haywire, become cornered or misdirected, other qualities, such as being ethical and evaluative (see discussion under Expecting Qualities), will control power.

In the examples above, the board responds positively to the petitioners' request. The board doesn't unilaterally come up with a decision but opens the process further throughout the church. In the second example, the building committee is expanded to include persons who are nearest to the information that is needed to design a quality nursery. These examples demonstrate that the qualities of listening, of being communicative, responsive, ethical, and of having high expectations are characteristics of high quality effective leadership actions.

➡ DIAGNOSTIC QUESTIONS **Is the full participation of laity built into the polity of the church?**

Do the members of the congregation have power? How many positions of power are occupied by laypersons? How many different laypersons are in positions of power?

Do they exert their power? In how many circumstances (task forces or committees) do laypersons make decisions? In how many ministry teams do they advise? In how many circumstances do they consult with the leaders before decisions are made? (Remember the goal of increasing these numbers by five percent per year.)

Is there a comprehensive program for training laypersons to do their jobs? Is there an established set of principles delineating requirements for all lay officers and workers to receive training? Is there a set schedule for continuous lay training?

What decisions does the congregation make as a unit? Does the laity participate in budget decisions? Do laypersons participate in worship decisions? Do they participate in program decisions? Do they participate in personnel decisions? Do they participate in administrative decisions?

How often do laypersons make these decisions? How often are members of the laity present when key issues are decided?

What absolute decision-making power is afforded the ordained leadership? List examples of how and when it is used.

➡ IMPLEMENTATION IDEAS   The pastor should communicate continuously in many different settings that the congregation supports the high-quality guidance offered by the laity. The board must be convinced to empower the laity in every area of the congregation's life and work. Meetings and discussions should be held to focus on increasing lay participation. Channels of influence and decision points should be delineated. A congregation organization chart should be flexible.

Training should be given on church organization and decision making. Other qualities, such as being communicative, having a sense of community and providing pastoral care will lead to increased sharing of decision-making power with the laity.

Young persons coming of age and new members are special concerns. Physically disadvantaged and identified minorities also need recognition for their abilities and decision-making knowledge. No incremental increase in lay participation will likely occur unless a special effort is made to guide the power of these persons into the polity.

Empowering the laity should never be discussed apart from training laypersons to understand their role and to do their jobs well. Talk of empowering the laity must always be followed by asking, "Empowering for what?" If persons are empowered and do not know how to use that power effectively, the end result will be more conflict than before. To empower a person to use firearms without giving the person training in the deadly power of a firearm and how to use it safely may result in injury or death—usually to others that one loves. To empower persons and groups to act, to make influential decisions, and to otherwise wield power, without training them to do their jobs well and how to use power appropriately, may result in serious injury to ministry and to the entire congregation. It is very easy to give power away. It is almost impossible to take power back once it is given. The single largest cause of conflict in churches is the music program; the second largest source of conflict is among empowered persons who have never been trained to use their power appropriately.

➡ **RESOURCE MATERIALS**   Troeger, Thomas H., and Carol Doran. *Trouble at the Table: Gathering the Tribes for Worship.* Nashville: Abingdon Press, 1992.

Wright, Timothy. *A Community of Joy: How to Create Contemporary Worship Services.* Nashville: Abingdon Press, 1994.

Wilson, Marlene. *How to Mobilize Church Volunteers.* Minneapolis: Augsbury Publishing House, 1983.

Larson, Carl E. and LaFasto, Frank M. J. *Teamwork: What Must Go Right/What Can Go Wrong.* Newbury Park, CA: Sage Publications, 1989.

3 - Gathering Qualities

THIS GROUP OF QUALITIES FOCUSES ON THE NUMBER, VARIETY AND INCLUSIVENESS OF THE CONGREGATION'S MINISTRY PROGRAMS.

➡ HAS MANY PROGRAMS
➡ OPEN MOST OF THE TIME
➡ COMMUNICATIVE

This group of qualities focuses on the number, variety and inclusiveness of the congregation's ministry programs. Churches of high quality tend to embrace people over time and space. To embrace people one must communicate with them. A church that has many programs and is open most of the time will have very little impact if the people are not aware of what is going on, or if the results of the ministries are not communicated.

The gathering qualities develop an opportunity for service. Service is related to and supportive of spirituality.

➡ GATHERING QUALITIES

➡ HAS MANY PROGRAMS

➡ DEFINITION   A high-quality church offers a menu of many ministries, programs, committees and social groups that positively involve most, if not all, persons in the congregation. The size of the menu is relative to the size of the church. A small church of 50 members can develop several opportunities for positive action, even if these opportunities are offered within one group that sets out to meet a specific need in their community. The important standard is to have enough activities to provide every person a variety of opportunities to "connect" with the church through involvement in one or more connecting groups that are meaningful to them. These groups may be ministry, program, committees or social groups. At a larger church there must be a broad variety to assure that there is something for everyone. A smaller church will likely do one or two things very well, which will define its mission and preserve its intent to have a variety of programs.

Ministries involve individuals in service to others. *Programs* are activities that educate and entertain. *Committees* are the formal structures to administer the business of the congregation. *Social services* cover all other activities. In many ways current trends are similar to those involving churches in centuries past. Over the centuries many functions, such as education and health care, were major church activities. Today we find clinics, day care, soup kitchens, sleeping quarters for the homeless, persons needing asylum and innumerable other activities being carried out by church ministry groups.

➡ EXAMPLES **The Quality Church Allows Choices for Children.** "You and your family attend church don't you?" commented George Adams to his friend Harry Glover as they enjoyed their lunch break together. "Our kids will be in the first and third grades this fall. We're thinking it's about time to find a Sunday school and church for them. Does your church have a good program for kids?"

"Alice and I think our church is a good place for our kids to be," responded Harry. "We think kids should have the opportunity to do what they want to do, and our church has a variety of excellent opportunities for kids of all ages. On Sunday mornings we have a variety of Sunday school classes and children's church. We also have excellent child-care services for those who are too young to be in group activities. Then throughout the week there are several programs and activities for the kids to choose from. Why don't you and your family come with us to church next Sunday? When your kids get there, someone in the children's department will describe the various opportunities available to them, and they can decide for themselves. There is no problem; the children will be welcome in whatever they decide to do."

Sixteen years ago, long before the advent of quality dawned upon churches, Tim and his family were traveling through Wisconsin and stopped in a small town to attend Sunday services. They found an inviting church situated on a well kept yard and decided to worship there. In the front of the church there were four parking spaces marked "Visitor." As Tim drove down the street a greeter stepped off the curb and motioned Tim to park there. Tim told him he could park in the parking lot across the street, but the man said, "These spaces are for our guests; please park here."

As Tim and his family got out of the car a person approached them, introduced himself, walked with them into the church and introduced them to a greeter. The greeter asked the children (not Tim or his wife), ages four and six, whether they would prefer to attend the service with their parents or to attend the children's program. The children said they wanted to be with the other kids.

The greeter then took Tim and his wife along with their two children to an area of the building clearly designated as the kids' area and introduced the children to the leader of the children's department. The children's leader positioned herself on the same level as the children and told them about the Sunday school classes they could attend and what would be happening in the classes that day, and also told them of a program they could attend if they chose not to attend a Sunday school class. The kids opted to attend the classes.

The greeter then accompanied Tim and his wife into the sanctuary and sat with them during the worship service. When the service was over, the greeter took them to the fellowship hall for coffee and introduced them to some other members. After they had finished their coffee, the greeter took them to their children and later walked with them to their car.

Not once in this entire experience were they asked to "stand up" to be introduced, or to sign a card or a book. They were never asked whether they lived in the community. When they got to the car, Tim commented to the greeter how greatly impressed they were with the hospitality and care shown them. The greeter said, "Our vision is to be a welcoming church, to make everyone feel at home. Every guest in our church is welcomed as you were. We want people to feel at home with us."

Today, sixteen years later, the church continues to grow. Its growth has never been very fast, but it has been constant over the years.

A Large Church Has Many Programs for Adults. The Saddle-back Valley Community Church, Lake Forest, California, has been built on the concept of providing multiple options in programs, small groups and events for adults. "We live in a world of thirty-one flavors of ice cream and fifty channel cable TV," says Rick Warren, the senior pastor. "To minister to people in the 1990s, we must look for niches and individual needs, and customize our programs to meet those needs. The idea of serving everyone the same thing doesn't work anymore." As a result of its attention to the differing needs and interests of persons, Saddleback Church ministers to about 20,000 people on a regular basis.

A Young Family Chooses a Church. We recently conversed with a young woman whom we met at a church where we were consulting. She and her family had recently chosen to attend this church, and she was anxious to tell us about it. "After we got married," she said, "Joe and I began attending the church in which we were married, but we stopped attending after a few years because it was just too boring and offered nothing to excite our commitment.

"Then last year, when our second child entered the second grade, we decided it was time to get back into church and Sunday school. We visited four churches before deciding to make this our church home. We were very concerned that the kids would like whatever church we attended, and so we listened carefully to what they had to say about each church we visited. For the other churches we visited, the kids either had nothing to say or they would ask, 'We don't have to go back there, do we?'

"Then we visited this church. Joe and I liked it from the moment we entered the building. We were especially impressed with the many programs the church offered for adults—things in which we could get involved. After the services, when we got in the car, the kids started talking about how much they liked the classes and the children's church they had attended, and they gave me a bulletin of programs in which they could participate during the week. Then they asked, 'Can we come here again next Sunday?' Joe and I just looked at each other and said, 'This is it.'

"I work in a program which prepares and serves meals to homeless and hungry people. Also I am presently taking a course in church history. The course is held on Tuesday evenings and is taught by a member of our congregation who is a college professor. The class offers college credit for those who want it. I am taking it for credit.

"Joe has become a member of a small group that meets monthly. The group emphasizes a daily routine of prayer and involvement of each member in a volunteer ministry. Joe likes to build things and has joined the Habitat for Humanity group in the church."

➡ COMMENTS   Although stories like these excite us, they no longer surprise us. The only surprising thing is that so many congregations have not yet learned the lesson that a *church of high quality has many programs for persons of all ages.* That fact poses a chicken-and-egg dilemma. On the one hand, it is easier to have many programs if the church is growing. On the other hand, however, no church will grow unless it has many programs. Which comes first?

Perhaps a church caught in the dilemma should set policies stipulating a minimum number of new programs to be started each year, and target an acceptable annual percentage increase in participation. Further, the church should invest some effort to discover the points of greatest opportunity for program and ministry expansion—and target these areas.

In *The Seven-Day-A-Week Church,* Lyle Schaller describes in one page "The Attractiveness of Choices":

> The vast majority of Protestant congregations on the North American continent offer people two choices: take it or leave it. "If you want to join us in the corporate worship of God, come when we gather, or don't come. If you want to sing in an adult choir or participate in a high school Sunday school class or share in an adult Bible study group, we offer only the one. Take it or leave it."
> . . . One church, for example, invites children from infants through age three to be in the nursery. Down the road a large full-service parish has one room for infants, another room for toddlers, a third room for children eighteen to twenty-four months old, a fourth room for those twenty-four to thirty months old, and a fifth room for children thirty to thirty-six months old. Which church do you think the mother of an eight-month-old or a twenty-month-old will choose?

... "Them that has, gits."[1]

To Schaller's pithy one liner we would add:

"If you always do
    what you've always done,
then you'll always get
    what you've always got."

➡ DIAGNOSTIC QUESTIONS **Is there the requisite variety of ministries, programs and committees to meet the needs of our congregation?** Some have suggested one group for every ten persons in the congregation.

How many ministries are there? Categorize the ministries by type. Count the number of people participating, hours in service or other measures.

How many programs are there? Who attends the programs? How many people attend each program?

How many committees are there? Who attends the committees? How many people attend each committee?

What is the ratio of groups to the number of persons who attend? Many congregations establish standards for the desired number of ministries, committees and programs, based on membership. What are the ratios of ministries to members? Committees to members? Programs to members? Committees to ministries?

What percentage of the congregation participates in ministries? Committees? Programs? The sum of all three percentages should ideally be 100 percent. Involvement in church activities is one hallmark of a high-quality church. If you have more people on committees than in ministries, you may already be in trouble.

How many ministers and paid staff are supporting ministries? Committees? Programs?

How much overlap in activities is there?

How much of an overlap of membership is there in the activities?

How many new ministries, committees and programs are added each year?

How many aging or worn-out ministries, committees and programs are eliminated each year?

Are the same people doing everything? Profile the activities of each congregation member. Then compare their profiles to see how participation might be spread.

➡ IMPLEMENTATION IDEAS   New activities and existing groups should be nurtured. The roster of activities should be regularly reviewed with an eye toward providing an increasing variety of opportunities for involvement. New activities should be regularly added to allow for greater numbers of persons to be connected and involved. As an activity or group outlives its usefulness, it should be disbanded to make room for new and more vibrant involvement opportunities.

Every three or four years each program should "go on the block for its life." These questions should be asked: (1) If we were not already running this program, would we start it now? If not, the program should be discontinued. If the answer is yes, then the program should be completely reviewed for possible changes to make it more fully effective—and put on the road for another three or four years. (2) Does the response to this program give us any ideas for other programs that should be started?

Simply having overlapping groups is not enough. These groups must be functioning well and providing a high-quality experience for the participant. Standards for quality in participation should be established and followed.

The need for standards is especially crucial for administrative committees and service ministries. Establishing high expectations of persons who serve in these groups will create a greater sense of value and meaning for the persons carrying out the activities. A standard crucial to success is *accountability*. By treating activities seriously, the leadership will strengthen the loyalty of the participants to the activity and ultimately to the church. As the activities and jobs carry more meaning, they will require more, not less, staff involvement (although by involvement we do not suggest more authority for the staff).

If you accept the standard of one group for every ten persons in the church, one would count prayer groups, hobby groups, alcohol and drug rehabilitation groups, classes, committees, boards, missions and so forth, so long as their existence were based on the desires and needs of the people, not the result of some theoretical, administrative fiat. Furthermore, group structure in a congregation should not be based on an arbitrary disciplinary standard within a denomination that assumes one structure or two structures will fit all or most congregations. The targeted needs of the people, from outside to inside, should creatively and flexibly govern the group structure or group process.

The creation of the group structure is actually one of common sense. Every interested person should be queried regarding their needs and interests. They should be encouraged to join one or more existing groups. New types of groups may emerge based on the members' interests. Little effort should be made to save groups in which members lose interest. There should be a constant generation of new activities to accommodate the numbers of persons attending the church, and their varied interests.

Formation and support of groups should be managed, most of the time, with lay leadership. The staff of the church would be overwhelmed if they were expected to care for and direct all of the groups. Some congregations hire a volunteer coordinator to make sure that the groups are improving participation rather than stifling it. Only in cases of serious conflict involving problems that would hurt the church should the staff (carefully) interfere.

Following are some suggested guidelines for the management of activities.

> Every leader must have a job description filed with the church board before being appointed to the leadership position. Task forces will not have job descriptions, because of their temporary nature. They will, however, be given a very clear assignment or mission. A higher-level body may set a job description for lower-level units.
>
> After three months a group leader must prepare a set of objectives for the group, or review or revise the existing set.
>
> Objectives may be added, deleted, or modified at any time after notifying the next-higher-level administrative body.

A group leader's job is to carry out the duties outlined in the job description and to meet the established objectives.

Each year a report will be submitted, by all committees, to be included in the church's annual report. Each leader must submit a self-assessment of his or her performance, measured against the objectives and the job description. These reports are not about budgets or things the group did, but about mission and results.

The church staff will be responsible to maintain records of job descriptions, group objectives, and yearly reports for each committee and group and to distribute them as appropriate. This requires that manuals and information, job descriptions, objectives, and other information be regularly submitted by the group leaders during each administrative period. Volunteers are to be recruited to maintain the materials and make them available to committees and their leaders.

Group leaders should be regularly rotated to increase participation. Rules made must be enforced to ensure regular turnover among the leadership. Careful planning can also create desirable continuity. For example, group leaders might serve for three- or four- year, nonrenewable terms. In the first year a person will be the leader elect, on the second year he or she will be the group leader, and serve as the leader emeritus during the third year. No one will be allowed to follow oneself in the same leadership position.

A recognition program that regularly features the work of volunteers is desirable. An honors banquet, recognition during services and pins to be worn are some of the obvious possibilities for recognition. A recognition program draws attention to exemplary service as a model for all members of the congregation. Recognition is also an opportunity for joy and fellowship.

➡ RESOURCE MATERIALS   Johnson, Douglas. *Empowering Lay Volunteers.* Nashville: Abingdon Press, 1990.
Schaller, Lyle. *Choices for Churches.* Nashville: Abingdon Press, 1990.
———. *The Seven-Day-A-Week Church.* Nashville: Abingdon Press, 1992.
Shawchuck, Norman, et al. *Marketing for Congregations: Choosing to Serve People More Effectively.* Nashville: Abingdon Press, 1992.

➡ GATHERING QUALITIES

➡ HAS MANY PROGRAMS
➡ **OPEN MOST OF THE TIME**

➡ DEFINITION   In a high-quality, comprehensive church ministry and program, no matter what its size, activi-
ties are offered at most times of the day and utilize most of the available space in the church buildings. This benchmark quality allows
churches to plan and schedule activities to match the varied sched-
ules of the members of the congregation. Church space is a
resource to which the finest stewardship should be applied. Lack of
space constrains persons and programs. Space that stands empty
and unused throughout the week indicates that ministry and program opportunities are continually being lost. Empty space may call
for programs. A church may choose a tapestry of activities in
response to its vision and mission. In that case the usage of church
space would be planned in light of the missional goals of the congregation.

➡ EXAMPLES   **Mark Blaising and Trinity Church, Elkhart,
Indiana.** For several years Mark Blaising served
as the pastor of Trinity United Methodist Church in Elkhart, Indiana.[2] There he set a high standard for quality in every aspect of the
church and its ministry, and he was never ashamed to utilize the
good will that was generated by the church's programs to attract
new people to the church.

During Mark's tenure as pastor, the congregation started a succession of programs aimed at serving the needs of young couples with
small children. It all began when the church started a Thursday
morning *Mother's Day Out* program for mothers with small children. The mothers could bring their children to the church and
leave them for several hours on Thursday, while they went out to do
whatever they wanted to do—shop, relax, go to a movie and the like.
The program was conducted by volunteers and paid staff from the

congregation. There was a minimal charge for leaving the children there.

After the Mother's Day Out program had been operating for several months, Mark polled all of the parents using it, asking them what they missed the most now that they had small children and their families were just getting settled in new homes, better jobs and different responsibilities. The overwhelming response from the young parents was that they missed being able to go out on "dates." They spoke of the times before they were married or before they had kids. They had a little more loose money then and could afford going out to a nice restaurant, or to the theater. But now, with the added costs of establishing a household and the responsibilities of caring for the little ones, it seemed they never had the time nor the money for a "date."

In response to this, the church launched a *Sunday Morning Brunch* for young parents. This affair emphasized a white table cloth with china and silver. There was always special entertainment during the brunch; a special music group, a drama group or public speaker of interest to parents. The church provided nursery services for the kids, so that parents could bring their kids with them to church and pick them up when the brunch was over. The church provided the brunch and entertainment to the young parents without cost.

After some time, the church launched a day-care program in addition to the nursery school for small children of working parents. The parents could bring their children while they worked at jobs in the Elkhart area.

Thus we see but one example of how Trinity Church started a program that lasted only for a few hours on Thursday and used it to launch other programs, finally resulting in programs for young families which utilized a great deal of space in the church building, and eventually utilized that space seven days a week.

In our opinion, what made these programs possess a special quality was the ability of the people at Trinity Church to focus on the needs of a particular group, and then go on from there to serve as a means of evangelizing the unchurched persons in that group. We met with many members and participants in the church. Several of them reported how they first used one of the programs of the church, and through it were attracted into full participation and membership.

Out of the Rental Business and into Ministries

One of Shawchuck's seminary classes included a student who was the pastor of a church in Illinois. He had been there about seven years. When he arrived, several programs and events were being carried on inside the church, but most of these events were run by groups who merely rented space from the church. The congregation primarily used the building space for its Sunday services—and the rest of the week rented out space, collected the rental fees and complained that the tenants didn't take enough care with the facilities.

He decided that this situation was detrimental to the life and ministry of the church and set about to take the church out of the rental business. Several members soon joined him in this effort. After all of the rental arrangements had been terminated, he set about encouraging the congregation to develop or sponsor church-related programs and services.

The newly available building space allowed the creation of a number of vigorous ministries run by various groups within the congregation. Each of the programs was spearheaded by interested ad hoc groups of members and nonmembers, and they all continue to be operated by these groups. Among the ministries are a soup kitchen, a training program for emotionally disturbed adults and a day-care center for children whose parents work in the downtown area surrounding the church. They also provide space for a budding African-American congregation.

➡ COMMENTS   Why would a pastor work through ad hoc groups to launch these ministries? Why wouldn't he plan through one of the standing committees, such as the missions committee or the social concerns committee? In *Strategies for Change*, Lyle Schaller asserts that a leader should not give new ventures to standing committees because standing committees are designed to preserve and manage what is already there. Standing committees are not good at creating something new or envisioning a different future. New ministries should be given to ad hoc committees that have only one clear mission: to plan and begin the new ministry.[3] Most good ideas never get off the ground once they are assigned to standing committees.

Bruce Ough, a district superintendent in the United Methodist Church in Iowa, thinks that the issue of rental or free-use space is not the most important issue. He wants to know, "Is this program an integral extension of the mission and ministry of our congregation?" If it is, Bruce suggests, then it should be kept—even if it brings no money to the church. If it isn't, he says, then it should be discontinued—even if it pays the church a fair rental fee.

Unfortunately, Bruce Ough finds that many pastors simply refuse to allow any social or community service program located in the church building to support the congregation's evangelism or marketing efforts. "It isn't that pastors don't know how to do this," he said. "Basically pastors resist any appearance of being interested in evangelizing or increasing participation among people in their church through the 'outside' activities that go on in the church. So the leadership treats the people who enter the building throughout the week as impersonal tenants, rather than seeking to know those who are unchurched, and then seeking to evangelize them."

If this attitude is widespread, and we think it is, then the quality of being open most of the time isn't simply a matter of how much and how often the building is used, but to what ultimate purposes. To make a little money, to provide space for needy causes or for worthy groups is not likely the benchmark for the use of the building and its facilities. However, to expand the ministry opportunities of the members and other people in the community, to seek to invite persons into a relationship with Christ and the church through the various activities that go on there—this is the benchmark of quality for use of the facilities.

So, one key to achieving the gathering qualities is to utilize the full potential of the church facilities, and the skills and commitment of the congregation to capitalize on the many ministry and evangelism opportunities presenting themselves to the church. The rationale for having many programs and having the church building open most of the time is to give every member and other interested persons opportunity to volunteer in significant ministries to the congregation and the community.

➡ DIAGNOSTIC QUESTIONS **Are there activities every day? How many are on site and off site?** Keep records of who uses space and how much they pay.

How much of the space is utilized daily? Develop tables of space usage by week, month and year.

What percentage of the activities are for noncongregation activities?

What percentage of the noncongregation activities are in line with the mission of the congregation?

What percentage of the noncongregation activities serve the church solely by bringing in additional revenue? How much money is raised? How many members participate in these activities? What does the opportunity cost? What ministry opportunities are lost because of these noncongregation activities?

What percent of the church budget comes from renting to noncongregation activities? The total amount and percentage of the annual budget met by rentals should be examined in the light of whether rental fees encourage or discourage financial stewardship.

➡ IMPLEMENTATION IDEAS Activities supported by the church should fulfill the mission of the church. Activities should be scheduled at several times and every day. Responsible and fair scheduling is important in most churches. If there is much surplus space, scheduling is not critical except to be fair to the users. Year-round calendars are the best way to implement scheduling. Extensive dissemination of calendar information and activities is vital. Some major events may have to be scheduled more than a year ahead. All key groups should participate in schedule development.

Scheduling should give priority to the following activities:

* Worship, prayer groups and support for worship and prayer groups (training, usher meetings, etc.). Music is an important component of worship, as well as being desirable for intrinsic reasons.
* Church administrative and management activities.
* Religious education for children and adults.
* Pastoral care by church staff, which includes support groups. A special consideration will arise with Twelve-Step groups, which are among the most common users of church facilities. Twelve-Step groups established to meet the needs of members of the congregation should clearly be given priority. If there is excess unused capacity, outside Twelve-Step groups could be allowed to use some of the space. But there must be a clear and stated willingness on the part of these groups to terminate their use if the space is needed for expanding church activities.
* Missional ministries, from soup kitchens to collection of food and clothing, are appropriate as long as there is significant involvement of church members.
* Social activities of members and church fellowship activities are weighed as a core activity.

Any activity that is a planned part of the church evangelization program is highly desirable use.

When weighing competing interests, use these suggested criteria:

* Importance to accomplishing the church's mission
* Numbers of persons who participate
* Equity among groups that have the same priority with respect to the church's mission. Each should be given equal access to building and time use. Lower-priority activities should be supported at lower levels.
* Available alternatives. For example, a teen group may have no alternative site, while a men's group may have several available venues.

➡ RESOURCE MATERIAL

Schaller, Lyle. *Choices for Churches.* Nashville: Abingdon Press, 1990.

———. *The Seven-Day-A-Week Church.* Nashville: Abingdon Press, 1992.

Shawchuck, Norman, et al. *Marketing for Congregations: Choosing to Serve People More Effectively.* Nashville: Abingdon Press, 1992.

➡ GATHERING QUALITIES

➡ HAS MANY PROGRAMS
➡ OPEN MOST OF THE TIME
➡ **COMMUNICATIVE**

➡ DEFINITION   In a communicative church, open and valid communication flows in all directions. Persons sending the communication assume responsibility for being understood. And, each communicator is responsible for making sure that the communication is effective. Communication covers organizational and individual information. Organizational communication often requires the use of media. The quality of sent messages and communications will intersect with most other qualities. Interpersonal communication especially requires additional concern for the qualities of believing, showing pastoral care and having high expectations.

➡ EXAMPLES   Conventional wisdom about organizational conflict seems to set the score as follows: 75 percent of organizational conflict stems from misunderstandings, and all misunderstandings are the result of poor communications. This estimate may be too high but it does accentuate the detrimental effects of poor communications upon relationships, trust and ministry in the church.

When All Ears Are Closed and No One Is Communicating with Anyone. Faith Church experienced a crisis that, due to poor communication, left it seriously, angrily divided into two camps. The camps were the young adults and new members vs. the elders of the church, all of whom were long-time members. The conflict was so destructive that serious consideration was given to closing the church, even though it had more than 175 members and an average attendance of about 125.

The conflict erupted shortly after a new minister arrived, when four young married women in the congregation and the church secretary complained that the pastor was making lewd comments and sexual advances toward them. The group of long-time, older members who had served as the pastoral search committee were adamant that the new pastor was doing no such thing, and that the secretary and the younger women in the church were simply trying to cause trouble.

Several people left the church. After about five months the secretary quit her job and filed suit against the church and the pastor for sexual harassment. The pastor immediately resigned the church, claiming he was being forced out by the young couples, who had convinced the secretary she should file the legal suit. Under mounting pressure, the elders retained the services of a church consulting agency.

The consultant visited with the secretary, who said she did not want to file suit but felt it was the only way she could get the congregation's attention. She indicated that if steps were taken to make certain sexual harassment did not continue on the part of the pastor, she would drop the suit. She stated further that at no time had the elders of the church communicated with her, in spite of her cry for help.

The consultant asked the elders whether they had communicated with the church where the pastor had previously served before hiring him. They had not, but, they informed the consultant, their judicatory executive had communicated with the judicatory official under which the pastor had last served, and the official had given the pastor high recommendations. The consultant urged the elders to make direct communication with the other church. They did so, only to discover that the pastor had left after similar allegations, and that they had failed to communicate this to their judicatory official because they had cut a secret agreement with the pastor in order to get him out quickly.

The elders shared the information with the search committee members. They dismissed the information out-of-hand, saying it simply could not be true. The consultant and a small group of elders then met with the older members and tactfully told them the entire story. The members responded that it simply was not true, that there was some sort of conspiracy afoot to destroy the pastor, that the pastoral search committee would never have called a pastor with these behaviors. Up until this time the older members had stead-fastly refused to talk with the young married couples regarding these matters. The judicatory executive had complicated the conflict further by telling all to keep the problem secret.

The decision was made to call a meeting of the entire congrega-tion. The consultant asked the young women to tell their stories to the elders. As the older members listened to the stories of the young women, and the young married couples listened to the shame of the older members, who were now afraid they would lose face in the church, a terrible eighteen-month rift was mended in a matter of two hours. Before the meeting ended, the congregation had autho-rized finances to pay therapeutic costs for the pastor to deal with his problems, and to provide financial support for the pastor's family until he was ready to take another pastoral appointment.

The elders then met with the secretary to inform her of these actions. She agreed to drop the suit against the pastor and church on the condition that the pastor would avail himself to the congrega-tion's offer. The secretary said, "All I wanted from the beginning was for the elders to listen to me so that I might do my job without fear of something terrible happening."

Communication Heals Many Wounds. In a large congregation on the West coast, an older woman wanted to teach the junior high Sun-day school class. The Sunday school committee, however, recruited a young woman, married for one year and six months pregnant, to teach the class. No conversations were held with the older woman to tell her why she was not selected.

About one month after the young woman had taken the class, the older woman burst into a Sunday class session and loudly informed the young woman she was unfit to teach the class and then demand-ed that her daughter leave the room with her. Within minutes of this episode the young teacher developed severe pains and was rushed to the hospital, where for nearly twenty-four hours it appeared she might lose her baby.

After the crisis was over, the pastor asked the older woman to meet with her and the young teacher. The older woman flatly refused, saying she was not sorry for what she had done because she was right. After three weeks and several attempts to get the two women together (and a heated debate with the older woman's husband), the pastor finally succeeded in bringing the two women together.

The young teacher expressed her dismay and anger at the other's behavior. It made no difference to her, she said, because the young woman was unfit to teach the class.

(Do you see [hear] that up until this time many words had been hurled back and forth, and across the parish? But there had been no communication. No one was hearing the other, and the older woman was certainly not assuming any responsibility for being heard.)

After several minutes of many words and missed communication—and some skillful intervention on the part of the pastor—the younger woman said, "Don't you care that I nearly lost my baby?"

"No," said the other. "I never could have a baby. All of my children are adopted. I'm so empty, because I could never have a baby, that I want to love and be with every child I see. Why should you have your own baby and all those lovely kids in the class also?"

Communication had finally occurred. Soon the two women were weeping and praying and affirming each other. This episode confirms that organizational conflicts are the result of misunderstandings, and all misunderstandings are the result of poor communications.

➡ COMMENTS These stories of real life provide compelling examples of the communicative quality. They suggest that storytelling is an excellent metaphoric mode of restoring broken communication. Consider how seriously Jesus took communication through stories in the biblical narratives. He was characterized as one who came telling parables and stories wherever he went.

Effective communications includes a listening component. A message must not only be spoken—it must also be heard. Recall from the discussion regarding the quality of being mission driven, where it was stated that many major communicators believe the mission of the institution must be communicated at least fifty times per year, using many different media, or the mission will not be "heard" by the workers.

➡ DIAGNOSTIC QUESTIONS **Does communication flow freely between clergy, staff and members?** When asked, do clergy, staff and members state that they withhold communication from the laity? Do clergy, staff and members limit with whom they communicate?

Is communication active and responsible? Is thought given to the content and form of communication? Is everyone invited to clarify communication and achieve understanding?

Is there an appropriate balance of written and spoken communication in the congregation?

Does every member receive significant communication at least once a month?

➡ IMPLEMENTATION IDEAS Communications training is one of the most important and available forms of education. Good communication requires communications skills and the motivation to communicate. In addition to having good communications skills there must be a level of satisfaction that good communication is occurring.

Good communication requires feedback. A process should be developed to assure that good (quantity and quality) feedback is occurring. Some churches have a tear-off portion of the weekly bulletin for communicating with the leaders. Others have comment forms or cards in the pews. In some congregations, each member of the board is a liaison to one or more constituencies in the church. Some churches set up neighborhood shepherding programs so that groupings of five to seven families know which designated leaders will listen to their concerns and, in well-conceived situations, minister to their needs. A suggestion/complaint box located in an easily accessible location can garner much feedback.

Having talk-back sessions after the public worship service is another way to increase communication. Some Episcopal churches formalize this as a Rector's Forum. Good communication is more likely when members are encouraged to participate in meetings, and where meetings occur at convenient times and in comfortable facilities. An annual canvas may be also used as an occasion to hear from all the members.

A communications committee might be established. The committee should be assigned to assess the amount and type of communication that exists. The committee may be able to fill some gaps in the overall communications process, and in other cases recommend how others might improve their communications. The committee might also offer communications training for groups or individuals.

Developing communications skills and learning how to share

A Communications Plan for Communicating a Tentative Vision Statement and Listening to the Congregation

Given that the church board has adopted a tentative vision statement, it should be clearly communicated to the members and others who attend the church.

* We need to notify the whole congregation.
* We need to do so as soon as possible.
* It is critical that people are presented with the statement more than once—they must hear it several times.
* A congregation meeting will be held.

Actions
* Have the pastor and board chairperson mention the vision statement and congregation meeting during Sunday services, beginning several weeks prior to the meeting.
* Call the board chairperson and set a date for the congregation meeting.
* Have a bulletin insert with the vision statement and information regarding the congregation meeting in the Sunday bulletin for several Sundays.
* Distribute the insert on the vision statement at all church activities.
* Include a story on the vision statement in the church newsletter. Check a draft of the story with the board chairperson and the pastor.
* Listening is important. Each board member should listen to the responses from the congregation. The responses should be summarized and reported to the board.

Continuing Actions
* Repeat the process with revised statements until the congregation and board agree on a final vision statement.

insights will also help members in their activities be-yond the church. The church, for many members, is a place to prepare for life on the job and in the home. Effective communication is one benchmark skill that is needed by everyone and everywhere.

➡ RESOURCE MATERIALS Kawasaki, Guy. *Selling the Dream.* San Francisco: HarperCollins, 1991.

Phillips, Donald T. *Lincoln on Leadership.* New York: Warner Books, 1992.

Recker, Burt. *You've Got to Be Believed to Be Heard.* New York: Morrow, 1991.

Tannen, Deborah. *You Don't Understand.* Valentine Books, 1990.

4 - Participative Qualities

THE TONE OF A CONGREGATION IS GREATLY
SHAPED BY THE PARTICIPATIVE QUALITIES.

➡ PASTORAL
➡ COMMUNITY

The tone of a congregation is greatly shaped by the participative qualities. A sense of pastoral care and community
support the congregation. Those who need care will
receive many benefits. Those who give care receive even
more benefits. Pastoral care extends beyond the congregation, to
outsiders, and even the staff. Pastoral care and a sense of community contribute to a sense of belonging, which will both attract and
retain members.

➡ PARTICIPATIVE QUALITIES

➡ PASTORAL

➡ DEFINITION   In a congregation characterized by pastoral
care, members of the clergy are known as persons
who genuinely care for people. Care is extended much more
through the identity of the pastor than through care-giving programs. The laity also reach out to those who need care. Care for and
of one another is a central tenet of Christian theology: "As we have
opportunity, let us do good to all people, especially to those who
belong to the family of believers" (Gal. 6:10 NIV). Developing a
pastoral feeling should not be solely the duty of the clergy or of a
specialized ministry in the church. Caring is by definition a way of
life for everyone who belongs to the community of believers.

➡ EXAMPLES **Caring for an Individual While Caring for the Congregation.** Recall from the discussion of "Guided by Lay Power" the story of a church where the music director's choice of music had grown out of date. A protest finally arose in the congregation, and the board moved to institute substantial changes in the type and styles of music in the worship services. We will now return to that story as an example of pastoral care.

The music director sternly resisted the intrusion into his territory, whether by members, pastors or church board. Upon hearing that changes might be called for, the music director made it clear that (1) he was not ready to retire and (2) when he did retire, he expected his son to take his place as music director.

The board realized it had no choice but to terminate the music director, after thirty years of faithful, if outdated, service. With the help of a consultant, the board prepared a plan that would achieve the necessary changes and, at the same time, be pastoral in its approach. The board realized that a pastoral approach in this instance required that they demonstrate genuine care for two different constituencies: the music director and those in the congregation who supported his traditional style of music, and those who were calling for changes.

The music director was sixty-three years old. The board appointed three of its members to meet with the music director to inform him (1) that the board had decided the time had come for him to retire, (2) that the new music director would be selected from outside the congregation, and (3) that the board had decided to hire a part-time music and liturgy assistant who would work with him and the clergy team to introduce new modes of music in the worship services and in other areas of the church.

Having said this, the group asked the music director three questions and requested that he meet with them in one week to give his responses. The questions were:

• Would you prefer to retire when you reach your sixty-fourth birthday (in which case we will pay you one year's additional salary), or would you prefer to retire when you reach age sixty-five?

- Do you wish to announce your retirement to the congregation, or do you prefer that the pastor or board chairperson do so? (They told him the announcement would be made in the Sunday services two weeks hence.)
- Do you wish to participate in planning your retirement ceremonies and festivities, or do you wish not to be involved? Are there two or three persons you wish to have involved in making these plans?

The following week the music director met with the group and gave his response to the three questions. At the appointed Sunday the announcement was made of his retirement—to occur at the time of his sixty-fifth birthday, a year and a half hence. At the following Sunday services the board announced its decision to hire a part-time music and liturgy assistant who would work with a special music committee and the music director to broaden the music menu of the church.

In this manner of expressing pastoral care for all persons, the board succeeded in effecting necessary changes without further conflict or anyone leaving the church. After his retirement the music director remained an active member of the congregation.

➡ COMMENTS   The benchmark quality of pastoral care underlines the importance of sensitivity in recognizing and responding to situations in which another person's feelings will be hurt or that the person might be publicly embarrassed, or that the ministry of the church might be impeded. Being pastoral requires that every effort be made to care for persons and groups— even when their needs or interests are antithetical. Again, although a group might be needed to coordinate the process of caring, this quality is not initiated by appointing a care-giving team such as a parish-life committee, but by becoming a holy people who genuinely care for one another. Even more important than developing the process of caring is forming the *character* of the congregation.

➡ DIAGNOSTIC QUESTIONS   **Does the congregation systematically reach out to its members and to all who call this their church?** Is the reaching out done by the clergy? Is the reaching out done by the lay staff? Is the reaching out done by members of the congregation?

Does the congregation systematically reach out to members and friends in need? How many times a year does a formal caring event occur? How many persons participate in caring? How many of the care givers are members of the clergy staff and how many are laypersons?

Is there an organized and effective process for discovering needs and scheduling outreach activities? Is there an outreach committee? How many members does it have? Does the committee do the caring or do they seek to involve others in the caring?

Does the laity care for the staff?

Does the staff care for the laity?

Does the congregation clearly care for strangers?

➡ IMPLEMENTATION IDEAS   In many churches, pastoral activities are considered the job of an ordained minister. In such congregations the pastor may be perceived as a family chaplain, or even a personal priest. In churches of high quality, however, pastoral care is everyone's job. This means that the pastor and staff need to learn how to set priorities and choose roles for themselves, but the greatest improvements will usually be made by encouraging lay participation. In pastoral activities, as with many other church roles, training is very important. The training will give confidence and set boundaries on the behavior of members. Persons are more spontaneous in caring if they know what is expected of them. Such training should help all members and staff to recognize where and when to refer to professional care givers. Congregations can develop lists of referral sources and make them widely available.

The offer of care is a delicate tight-rope walk; it is too easy to fall from real empathy into paternalistic domination. Persons are best treated by offering care and letting them accept or reject it. Many reasons come to mind why pastoral activities or intrusions might be rejected, and some have great merit.

A care-giving team may be useful for many reasons. The care-giving team may run or coordinate care-giving training. Because care is already part of the character of your congregation, probably the most important role of a caring team is to know who needs care at any time. The committee should also follow up to make sure that care is offered. The committee may do all the caring, but, at the risk of overstating, it is recommended that a caring team encourage many members of the congregation to participate.

Apart from the formal caring system, pastoral caring should also be an informal, ongoing activity. One-to-one interactions may at any time elicit caring. Ongoing groups, such as prayer groups, men's groups, spirituality groups, women's groups, Twelve-Step groups, may all meet major caring functions. Religious education courses, if taught in a participative manner, may also be the occasion for caring.

In recent years several large or informal studies have inquired into the major expectations and desires that laity hold for their clergy. All of these studies have highlighted the desire for a pastor who cares for the laity, quite apart from structured care-giving programs. For example, the newly appointed bishop of Eastern North Dakota, Evangelical Lutheran Church of America, surveyed people at eight conference assemblies asking what they thought was most important for the bishop to be doing. The top four responses were inspire, encourage, love and pray. Administer, minister, teach and lead came in twelfth, twenty-second, twenty-third and twenty-fourth places respectively.[1]

➡ **RESOURCE MATERIALS**   Ewers, Duane A. *A Ministry of Caring.* Nashville: Discipleship Resources, 1983.

Marshall, Maxine. *How We Become a More Caring Congregation.* Nashville: Discipleship Resources, 1981.

Stone, Howard W. *The Caring Church.* New York: Harper & Row, 1983 (available in libraries).

Sunderland, Ronald H. *Getting Through Grief: Caregiving by Congregations.* Nashville: Abingdon Press, 1991.

Zapp, Diane and William Dixon. *Lay Caregiving.* Minneapolis: Fortress Press, 1982.

➡ PARTICIPATIVE QUALITIES

➡ PASTORAL
➡ COMMUNITY

➡ DEFINITION The high-quality congregation acts as a family, or as a neighbor in the community, in the best sense. Community in the life of the congregation has two foci: (1) the congregation's life together and (2) its relationships to the community in which it is located and serves. A low-quality church looks to the community to serve *its* needs through such things as free advertising, discounts on purchases and so on. High-quality congregations, whether large or small, have reversed this mind-set and are constantly searching to discover new ways to serve rather than to be served.

➡ EXAMPLES **Community Before Congregation.** Twenty-one years ago, Dale Galloway decided to start a church in Portland, Oregon by forming small groups of less than ten people. Then, when the small group concept was firmly established, he linked up the network, creating the church. He reasoned that he did not want to build a congregation of people who gathered once or twice a week to worship, or attend a meeting—and then scatter until the next meeting. He felt called to create a strong sense of community among persons—community that would draw persons into close bonds of genuine mutual care and support.

New Hope Community Church now has 6,000 members with approximately 5,500 people participating in small groups each week. It is in the small groups that pastoral care, evangelism, shepherding and discipling take place. In these groups, people become a caring family, or community, for one another. The groups live up to the name "TLC (tender loving care) groups."

The church strongly urges all of its members to belong to a small group and works consistently to make this happen. However, the staff recognizes that people must be free to choose whether they will be in a group and to which group they will belong. Persons are not assigned to groups. Rather, the staff works with them to find the group best suited to them. The philosophy of the church is to focus on building leaders who build groups.

Three things are required for membership in New Hope Community. The new member must (1) commit her or his life to Jesus Christ, (2) live by the Bible, and (3) attend a pastor's class, which is an orientation to membership. Eighty percent of the members did not belong to a church prior to affiliating with New Hope Community Church.

Community Building with Schools and Unlikely Young People. One of the most encouraging community-building ventures we have heard of in the past year was told to us by the youth ministry team at First Assembly of God Church in Santa Ana, California, where Albert Vaters is the senior pastor.

The congregation numbers 1,200 in Sunday worship attendance. The congregation has historically been Anglo. In recent years, however, the congregation has added many people from various ethnic backgrounds. This change was largely due to the cultural change in the community of Santa Ana and the influence of the youth department in the church.

As the community changed, the traditionally Anglo youth program dwindled. Pastor Vaters and the church board decided that the old ways would not work anymore and something had to be done. As a result, a young man, Norb Kohler, recently graduated from Southern California College with a master's degree, was hired as youth pastor. Norb had already gained a reputation for his aggressive community and high school outreach ministry. He immediately established contact with the Santa Ana and Orange County school boards and was appointed to the Santa Ana 2000 Gangs and Drugs Committee.

Two years later, the congregation brought two interns onto the youth ministry staff. The two young men were master's level students at Southern California College. The interns were given free rein to build a strong and growing youth ministry in Orange County. Norb and the two interns quickly established themselves as volunteer drug counselors and peer assistance leadership directors on the high school campuses of Santa Ana.

As a result, they have had opportunity to speak to over 30,000 young people on the high school campuses of Santa Ana. This opened the door to minister to several thousand young people involved in gangs and drug activity. Other high schools in Orange County took notice and invited them to establish gang and drug programs on their campuses.

Out of these efforts, many hundreds of gang and "at risk" students have become interested in living a different life-style with the help of Christ, Bible study programs and youth activities in a gun-free and drug-free environment.

Currently, the ministry serves 300 young people on a weekly basis, and annually has the privilege of sharing a message of hope with thousands of young people in the Orange County schools. The congregation is presently planning for the construction of a large multi-purpose youth center for the young people of Santa Ana and Orange County. This step will broaden the scope of community building among the youth, the congregation, the schools and social agencies in the area.

This story is a sterling example of a congregation reaching out to establish community with the school system, legal agencies and youth of different social, economic and ethnic backgrounds.

➡ COMMENTS The stories of building community in the examples given above are very different, but also valid and important reminders that the church is to be a community— and is also to foster community, within and without its own circle of persons. It grieves us to realize that too many congregations seek to build a protected community within, but abstain from outside community contact except to change it, evangelize it or beg from it—but rarely to serve it.

➡ DIAGNOSTIC QUESTIONS **Do the members of the congregation care for each other?** Do they serve each other? Do they spontaneously assist and care for each other, apart from formalized care-giving programs?

Does the congregation care for the regional community? Does the congregation seek to foster and support a sense of community across the local area? Is the congregation known for its concern for the welfare of the community?

Are there good intergenerational relationships? Are there intergenerational events or activities? What is the purpose and focus of these events or activities?

Are activities provided for each significant generational group: children, adults, seniors, marrieds, etc.? Is each group serving and being served?

Are all members dealt with in fairness and compassion? Is innovation praised? Is eccentricity accepted and supported?

➡ IMPLEMENTATION IDEAS   Community is not developed in a vacuum. Attendance at many activities, groups, classes and services builds community. The characteristics of having many programs and being communicative, discussed previously, support community. Ideally, every member should regularly attend services and church functions as well as belonging to at least one small connecting group. All of the members should be serving others in one way or another. Community occurs because of individual connections.

New members who are inducted through a membership or inquirers class have a built-in community. Every church leader knows how important it is for new members to know somebody or have someone who knows them. Knowing other members leads new members into structured ways of belonging.

MENTORING PROGRAMS

Mentoring programs will help integrate new and prospective members and build community. A prospective member who shows some interest should be assigned a mentor. Organizationally, membership development should be in the same organization as is the new-member integration function.

Seven important functions need to be carried out for new members:

• Determining the interests of the new or potential member.
• Incorporating the new member into some ongoing group, committee or activity. These might include the choir, the men's group,

putting children into Sunday school, the buildings and grounds committee, and so on.

• Introducing them to current members with like interests.

• Integrating them theologically and organizationally into the congregation. They should be encouraged to take appropriate classes and be given good political and practical hints about how to succeed in the church.

• Developing information on the new members and distributing it to various church activities. This helps the activities reach out to and integrate the new members.

• Checking up on members if they are not seen around the church. Any person who misses church two Sundays in a row should be contacted. If someone misses three Sundays in a row, they should be considered on the road to becoming inactive—every effort must be made to bring them back.

• Some churches have each "class" of new members go through a program together. This builds cohesion and belonging. The new members immediately have a group of friends in the church.

Work parties and projects may be great community builders. A shared working experience builds bonds between the participants. Is it not said that giving is better than receiving?

Any type of successful small group experience builds community. Courses, seminars, prayer groups, committees and retreats are just some community-building events.

Retreats are very powerful experiences in building community. Retreats may be run for spiritual, educational or general community building and fun. Retreats may have many diverse groupings of participants. Retreats, however, are relatively expensive. Some costs may be saved by finding religious, educational and community organizations that run reasonably priced retreat centers. A scholarship program is always welcome.

Meals are wonderful occasions for building community. The cost of meals may be daunting. Many churches have a potluck tradition, which does decrease costs. Some churches have members sign up for a pot-luck dinner program. A committee assigns persons to parties on the agreed-upon dates. Parties are held at the homes of members. This is a good way to keep meeting new people every year. The book of Luke is often referred to as a *meal theology,* because Luke lays much emphasis upon the fact that good things happen whenever people sit down to eat with one another, when Jesus is also at the table.

Child care always is an essential ministry if you hope to attract young married couples. It is a self-perpetuating mistake to say, "We will provide child care if young families begin to participate." They never will. Provide child care whether it is needed or not, and after a while young families will begin to participate. *This is one unforgettable benchmark of quality in the church: Never wait to provide a service until it is needed if your mission is to reach a specific segment of the community.* If a young mother arrives for an activity and there is no child care, you waited too long. She will likely not be back again.

Therefore, community-building programs will not bring about the desired quality if pursued as isolated events or experiences. Once again, quality is attributed to the congregation that sustains and continuously enhances

EXTENDED FAMILIES

Extended families are a special churchwide community-building program. An extended family is a group of fifteen to twenty-five individuals who become a family. What being a family means is determined by the participants. The definition is best evolved over time as the family gets to know each other.

Families might meet a few times a year for a potluck dinner or an outing. Or they might share pizza, watch a video, and then have a discussion of the film. They might choose to carry out joint projects to help members, or individuals might help other members of their family.

The purpose of the family is not to strengthen and perpetuate existing cliques. Some neutral person or group, such as the staff, might divide the interested participants into families. Some families might be intergenerational and others not. Not everyone in the family will necessarily be to one's liking. It is generally thought that in a real family there is always a strange relative. Appreciating and learning how to get along with "difficult" persons is an important skill.

the sense of community among its members and that works to improve relations with the world outside its core public.

➡ RESOURCE MATERIALS

Peck, M. Scott. *The Different Drum: Community Making and Peace*. New York: Simon and Schuster, 1987.
Vanier, Jean. *Community and Growth*. New York: Paulist Press, 1989.

5 - Outside-In Qualities

TO RELATE TO THE WORLD THE CHURCH MUST FIRST LISTEN AND THEN BE RESPONSIVE TO WHAT IT HEARS.

➡ LISTENING
➡ RESPONSIVE

To relate to the world the church must first listen and then be responsive to what it hears. These two qualities of listening and being responsive characterize outside-in thinking. Instead of prejudging out of hand what the world thinks, the congregation learns how to read the culture, listen to its needs and relate to its struggles. On the one hand, the congregation may and often will listen, then choose not to respond to what it hears. On the other hand, being responsive requires hearing what is being communicated. Or to put the matter in theological terms, a congregation will lack a persuasive apologetic if it is not aware of the world around it. Listening and responding to persons is a benchmark of a quality church.

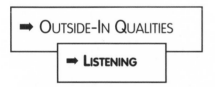

➡ OUTSIDE-IN QUALITIES

➡ LISTENING

➡ DEFINITION   In a listening church, the worship services, educational programs and all ministry activities routinely focus on hearing the ongoing needs, problems and possibilities within the congregation and the world. The congregation lives in a dynamic and changing world. The facts and assumptions of yesterday will undoubtedly change. The listening church knows what is going on within the congregation, the community and (to some extent at least) the world.

➡ EXAMPLES **Listening Through the Principle of Death and Resurrection.** The leaders of the church can listen with more avenues than their ears. God created us with five physical senses and intuition. Each of these gives us a unique contact with the world around us; each is a means of receiving communications that are sent our way. Your church can learn to listen with all of its senses. Following is an example of listening with several senses at the same time.

One of the authors (Shawchuck) attended a seminar led by Peter F. Drucker, along with a friend when both were fresh out of seminary. They were the only members of the clergy present. Everyone else was an executive in some financial or industrial corporation.

For three days the budding pastors were quiet and intimidated by the powerful executives who seemed to know so much. But on the third day, as the seminar ended, they pushed their way forward to touch Mr. Drucker before he left the room.

They presented themselves to the great teacher. "Mr. Drucker, we are both just out of seminary and are serving our first churches. You said a great deal to help us in our new jobs, but it's hard for us young guys to translate what you've said about running a large corporation so that it applies to running a small church. Tell us, Mr. Drucker, how would you summarize your teaching in this seminar for us as pastors?"

Mr. Drucker thought for a while, and then said, "I can summarize it for you in the principle of death and resurrection." Both pastors waited, wondering what in the world he might mean by this. Then he continued.

"You fellows go home and look around everywhere in your church. Wherever you see a ministry or activity that's showing strong signs of wanting to die—something where all interest and energy is draining away, something that seems to grow weaker even though you increase your efforts to resuscitate it—then you should assist this program to die with dignity. This," he said, "is the management principle of letting die what wants to die.

"And wherever you see a ministry or hear an idea that is trying to be born—you hear three or four people talking about it in different places, or the idea keeps coming up in committee meetings—you should act as midwife and bring these new ideas and ministries into life. When you do this, you put the church into the stream of God's action in the congregation. This," he said, "is the management principle of bringing to life what wants to be born.

"It is by the process of letting tired and weakened ideas and programs die that you generate energy and gain resources for new ideas trying to be born." Then he said, "And that's a good management plan for people who believe that God brought his greatest idea of all into reality through the principle of death and resurrection."

A Congregation Listens to Its Community. In rural northwest Ohio a church sits on a crossroad. There are only two houses and the church—nothing else. The congregation once flourished, but dwindled to sixty-five people, served by a retired, seventy-eight-year-old, part-time pastor. The community also declined as the farms became larger and larger, and the population smaller and smaller.

The part-time pastor said to the congregation, "If all you do is survive, you might as well close up." They thought about it and realized their church building was the only public building still open within an eight-mile radius. So they asked, "What happens if we close?" Then they created a plan.

First, they sent a letter to every resident living within the eight-mile radius, inviting them all to a potluck dinner to be provided by the congregation, with a community discussion following.

A week later they sent a flyer to every home in the eight-mile radius announcing the meeting and dinner. They posted fliers in every grain elevator, store and filling station left in the community. The week before the meeting they made personal visits in groups of two to every home, inviting the entire family to the church meeting. On the day of the meeting virtually everyone living in the eight-mile radius showed up.

After the dinner they asked the people to stay in their table groups and discuss the question, "What is the most important issue facing our community?" There were six table groups. When the table groups were asked to report, every one of them said, "What this community needs most is a place and reason to meet." The congregation asked how they might serve this need for the community. The table groups thought for a while, and then said, "Have more potlucks, and we will come. We need to do this in order to continue as a community."

The congregation listened to the community's words and decided if they could become the source of community for a scattered, rural people, they had found reason enough to keep the church open. They began to serve four community dinners per year, and the community folk came—and continue to come.

On the Sunday following the first dinner, in which the congregation listened to the community, there were ten new people in church.

The presbytery took notice of the congregation's attempts to listen and respond to their community. It authorized a redevelopment "probe" to help the congregation discover how it might market and serve the community in other new and important ways—even beyond the community dinners.

The church continues to grow as the centerpiece of "community" in the region. When this story began, every member of the church was over sixty years of age, except for one young family with one child. Now there are children and a Sunday school. The congregation has recently requested that the presbytery supply them with a full-time pastor. They now feel they can afford a full-time pastor without financial assistance from the presbytery.

➡ COMMENTS God created us with five physical senses and intuition. If you or your church leaders listen only with your ears, you may be receiving only about fifteen percent of the communication your congregation, the community and the world are sending your way. How much more might the principle of death and resurrection be effective among us if we were to bring ourselves to "listening" with our taste, smell, touch and vision?

For the pastor, one of the best methods of receiving communication is *listening while wandering around*. Pastoral home visitation has disappeared with the loss of neighborhoods and communities—and this void is a primary cause of many congregations feeling un-listened to, un-heard and estranged from the pastor and the church staff. Jesus had none of the resources made possible by computer technology and modern research to "listen" to the people, and yet all who met him left feeling they had been heard and understood. His listening method was one of the best—he listened while wandering around.

Listening can be done in many ways. It is not limited to listening to a spoken verbal communication. One can "listen" by observing behavior patterns, conducting questionnaire surveys, intuiting, and so on. However, all other types of listening should be supported by face-to-face communication whenever possible—and in the congregation this is always possible.

Listening begins at home and with groups most intimately associated with the church. It expands to groups and conditions around the world. Listening supports the communicative and the responsive qualities.

➡ DIAGNOSTIC QUESTIONS **Are the staff and congregation regularly and systematically kept informed about the world?** Is the staff well informed about local and world issues? Are there courses, seminar series or other events where members of the congregation can study or hear about events? Is there an alert system for important occurrences?

Do the staff and congregation listen to all relevant parties in the church? Who listens to members of the congregation? How are the nonmember regular attendees heard? How often are the members and attendees heard? Where are they heard? Is the information distributed, as well as recorded?

Do the staff and congregation listen to the local community? Does the congregation listen to all parties and community groups regarding important matters? Do members of the staff or congregation belong to key community organizations? If so, which? Are exchanges made with other organizations for listening purposes?

Do the staff and congregation listen to the rest of the world? Who on the staff is involved in listening to the issues from the rest of the world? How do they do it? To what organizations do they belong to keep up with the world?

➡ IMPLEMENTATION IDEAS A listening congregation needs to be informed. Local, national, international, as well as judicatory (when applicable) and denominational news should be followed. The pastor should give sermons addressing key issues and opportunities. Study groups should be regularly formed around problems and opportunities. The religious education program should present local and world issues for discussion and application of religious ideas. The ethical dimension of issues should be discussed.

There should be decisions within the congregation to set priorities as to where church effort will be placed. Social action should center on those issues that receive the highest priority. Special interest groups may be formed around issues that do not receive overall congregational priority.

One approach is to have a committee develop a list of key issues and opportunities that the church might address. A description of each of these would be prepared on a ballot. The congregation would rank these issues. The results would be presented to the congregation. Task forces can be formed around each item, as persons volunteer. The task forces that gather a sufficient complement of members become an active program.

An interpretative newsletter could be prepared. It would alert members of the congregation about breaking issues. It could also remind members of the congregation about issues in which the congregation has taken a stand, interest, or involvement.

Despite the typical suspicion about the national denomination's agencies, many congregations realize that well-planned and worthwhile denominational programs are often successful. A high-quality church will consider the best ideas and support them in light of its own mission and programs.

An informed listener will do better than a naive listener. Not knowing the language, background or concerns of a target group will make it difficult to hear their concerns. Preparation by studying appropriate books and magazines, watching movies and videos and speaking to informants is a good place to start. Informants are friendly persons who can tell you about a group or individual before you speak to them. For instance, speaking to your alderman about the mayor and to a college professor about a special group in his or her field of study are ways to begin preparation.

The listening groups should also be listening to each other. Listening must be done in an open and accepting manner. One should

A Listening Classification

The first task is to develop a list of who should be listening and who should be heard.

LISTENING GROUPS	GROUPS TO BE HEARD
Clergy	Neighbors
Paid staff	Ex-members
Volunteer staff	Government leaders
Board or Trustees	Other churches
Committee and organization heads	Judicatory officials
Members of committees	Denominational officials
Members of organizations	Social agencies
Members of the congregation	Businesses
Members of the community	Special groups

not argue or contradict. One should reinforce speakers by appreciating that they are giving time to you. It does not mean you must agree with what they are saying. Supportive feedback is important while you are listening. You need to convey to the speaker that you are listening. It might be a nod or a simple statement. Better feedback occurs if you can say something that ties in with the ongoing conversation.

Recording the conversation is vital. The date and name of participants should be noted. Depending on the conversation, one might take notes or record the conversation. In other cases it might be best to write down the notes immediately after leaving the conversation. Information then needs to be summarized and reviewed.

Meeting with others to compare and digest ideas is very important. Once the report is prepared, it should be presented and distributed to all interested parties.

➡ RESOURCE MATERIALS   Gordon, Thomas. *Parent Effectiveness Training.* New York: P. H. Wyden, 1970.

Lindgren, Alvin and Norman Shawchuck. *Let My People Go: Empowering Laity for Ministry.* Leith, ND: Spiritual Growth Resources, 1973.

Shawchuck, Norman, et al. *Marketing for Congregations: Choosing to Serve People More Effectively.* Nashville: Abingdon Press, 1992.

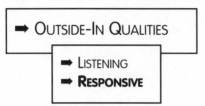

➡ OUTSIDE-IN QUALITIES

    ➡ LISTENING
    ➡ RESPONSIVE

➡ DEFINITION   A responsive congregation listens and responds to what is heard inside and outside the church. Being responsive must occur at two very important but different levels: A church must be responsive to its own staff and congregation, as well as responsive to the outside world. The outside world has several levels for consideration: potential members, the immediate community, the greater community of like organizations and denominations and the world at large.

➡ EXAMPLES   **Not All Churches Are Responsive.** In the days when horses were the primary beasts of burden in rural America, after several fine animals were presented to the crowd at a horse sale, the auctioneer would have an old, haggard, emaciated nag paraded before the crowd—so that they could better appreciate a good horse when they saw one.

Throughout this book we have told you many stories of high-quality congregations, both large and small. Perhaps by now it is becoming difficult to appreciate a high-quality church when you see one. Consider a nonresponsive, low-quality church, so that you may better recognize a responsive, high-quality church when you see one.

This story was told to us by a regional executive of an older denomination. Joe was invited by a congregation in his judicatory to preach on Sunday morning and to meet with the board following the service. The persons who made the contact did not give Joe an address or instructions for how to find the church.

As Joe approached the town he saw five church spires rising above the buildings. He drove to each of them, only to discover that none of them marked the church he was looking for. He then asked for directions to the church.

The church property had no sign, and nothing to indicate what denomination of which it was a part. Joe arrived fifteen minutes before the service was to begin. The building was locked and no one was in sight. Five minutes before the service was to begin an old man came down the sidewalk and unlocked the door. Joe got out of his car and walked inside, but the old man was nowhere to be seen. Joe sat down and waited. At one or two minutes before the starting time, approximately twenty-five people entered and sat down. No one approached to ask his name or to greet him.

The church organist arrived and Joe asked him, "How do you want me to conduct the service?" He answered, "I don't know; just do whatever you want." Joe asked whether any hymns or prayers had been selected. He said, "No, just use whatever you want."

At the final benediction everyone except the members of the board got up and walked out. Not one person spoke or greeted Joe. The board then sat down with Joe and asked, "We want you to tell us, why aren't we growing?"

A Responsive Church: Serving to Meet a Need. Earlier we said that the quality "community" is tied to serving others. Following is an example that demonstrates how being responsive is an essential ingredient of community building, whether inside or outside the congregation.

Boena Ridge church is a rural congregation that decided to search ways to be responsive to the needs of its community. At the beginning of this story the church had thirty kids in Sunday school and sixty members. There were eight hundred people within a five-mile radius of the church. The church building sits on a large and beautiful piece of property. The congregation could not afford to pay a pastor, so it was served on Sunday by a student from a nearby seminary.

The congregation grew bored with their routine and decided to take on a challenge to keep them alive beyond mere survival. They divided the community into zones and sent a few people into each zone to ask the residents what the church could do that would be of help to them personally or to the community at large. The people said, "You could build a playground for the kids." The community had no safe and stimulating place for the kids to play.

So the congregation built a large and beautiful community playground on their property. They did not ask anyone to help them and they asked for no contributions from the community. However, as the playground construction progressed, persons from the community began showing up to help with the construction.

Attendance at the Sunday services is growing. In April 1993, the congregation requested that the denomination provide a half-time pastor for two years, at which time they will consider calling a full-time pastor.

➡ DIAGNOSTIC QUESTIONS **Are the church's activities and ministries in tune with current issues?**

What level of social action is communicated to the outside community? How many social action projects are receiving support? How many participants are there in each program? How much money is committed? How is this money raised? What percentage of the church budget is allocated to responsive ministry?

What are the social action activities?

How many members are involved in social action activities? Who are the members that participate? Is there a subset of "social action types" who do everything? Is the whole church involved?

Does the congregation act to meet the expressed needs which they find appropriate to its mission? How are these needs found and presented? Who in the congregation decides on participation?

Are the worship services, ministries and behaviors of the congregation directed toward appropriate needs and opportunities?

➡ IMPLEMENTATION IDEAS Despite legitimate fears that social issues will polarize a community, the potential for conflict can be managed positively if the leadership seeks a congregation-wide involvement in setting priorities as to where church effort will be placed. Social action should center on those issues given the highest priority by the congregation at large,

OUTSIDE-IN QUALITIES / 111

which means that some church leaders may not be able to use their pulpits to bully the congregation into a single point of view. Special interest groups may be formed around issues that do not receive strong general support within a congregation.

One approach is to follow the procedure described under the quality of "listening." Have a committee develop a list of key issues that the church might address. A description of each of these issues would be prepared and distributed. The congregation would discuss these issues and rank them in order of priority, and also be able to add to the list. The results would be presented to the congregation. Task forces would be formed around each item as persons volunteer. The task forces with a sufficient complement of volunteers become active ministry teams.

Training may be required to prepare church members for mission. They need to have mental and behavioral training in how to be responsive.

Responsive congregations also rely heavily on the qualities of communicating and listening. A responsive congregation must have a highly informed leadership, lest the congregation be swept along in a sort of mob hysteria. Demographic studies, surveys, focus groups and secondary sources supply information that can help ensure responsiveness to reality.

In this section we have emphasized the importance of the quality of listening to being responsive. Communication requires a connection between two or more people.

→ RESOURCE MATERIALS Lindgren, Alvin and Norman Shawchuck. *Let My People Go: Empowering Laity for Ministry.* Leith, ND: Spiritual Growth Resources, 1973.
Schaller, Lyle. *The-Seven-Day-A-Week Church.* Nashville: Abingdon Press, 1992.
Shawchuck, Norman, et al. *Marketing for Congregations: Choosing to Serve People More Effectively.* Nashville: Abingdon Press, 1993.

6 - Expecting Qualities

ASIDE FROM RELIGIOUS AND LAY-LED QUALITIES,
THE EXPECTING QUALITIES ARE MOST IMPORTANT

➡ ETHICAL
➡ HAS HIGH EXPECTATIONS
➡ EXCELLENCE
➡ EVALUATIVE

A side from religious and lay-led qualities, the expecting qualities form the most important group of qualities. Holding expectations for high-quality effort in every undertaking, large and small, will greatly support and strengthen all the ministries and programs in the church.

One dissatisfaction that has driven people away from churches in the past two decades is disappointment with mediocre leadership and programs. A relational person with integrity, who embodies the highest benchmarks of ethical behavior, is the kind of leader that is respected by other clergy and laity.[1] In part, an individual's integrity is evidenced by being faithful and trustworthy to oneself.

A congregation reaches for high quality when its members strive to be transparent (honest) and whole. Moral values are the standards for being faithful and trustworthy to others. A congregation exists for the greater good through the proper application of high moral standards. In the rhetoric of quality, we may say that integrity comes from having a high-quality relationship with oneself. Ethical standards emerge from practicing, or living in, high-quality relationships with others, including and especially God.

Today, excellence is expected in all walks of life. Churches are not exempt. The commitment to do better has a long tradition. Scriptures always and everywhere call upon us to give our best and our all in service to the Lord. Can you imagine Jesus saying to the eager young man, "I realize you have many other things in your life which, at this point in time, may be more important than following me. Why don't you take all the time necessary to consider my call? Take your time. When you are older and have fewer obligations, then perhaps you can give the leftovers to me. I want you, but I certainly don't want to put you under any obligation . . .

"What's that you say? You don't have time just now to follow me, but you do have time to teach a children's Sunday school class. Yes, I understand, with your many other responsibilities you won't have much time to give to study and class preparation. That's okay; after all, they're just little kids. They're easily entertained. They don't know the difference between a good lesson and a sloppy one, and I'm sure your lack of preparation will have absolutely no influence whatsoever upon their decisions to stay away from church and Sunday school when they get older." (See Luke 9:57-62.)

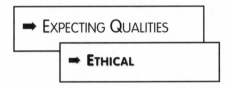

➡ EXPECTING QUALITIES

➡ ETHICAL

➡ DEFINITION An ethical church makes decisions based on Christian values and its vision for the future. Morals are based on a set of values that grow out of one's beliefs. Ethical choices must be made when values or interests are in conflict, especially when an individual's needs are in conflict with larger or corporate moral values. For example, stealing money from the Sunday school offering would meet a selfish need, but it is in conflict with a moral belief, "You shall not steal."

➡ EXAMPLES **Bearing Mutual Responsibility for Eroding Relationships.** A congregation of 1,500 members called a pastor who previously had served much smaller churches. The pastor was known for his ability to start a church or come to a small existing congregation and grow it to several hundred in a short while. The congregation was attracted to the pastor's vitality and get-things-done approach to ministry.

Within two years of the pastor's coming, the church was in great conflict, and relationships had badly eroded between the pastor and the ruling committees of the church. Much of this was due to the pastor not realizing that leading a well-established church was very different from starting a church or leading a young, rapidly growing congregation of five hundred or fewer members.

The congregation, pastor, denominational officials and a third-party consultant worked together to assess the situation. From the beginning, everyone agreed this was a no-fault situation; everyone had acted in good faith and yet had failed to anticipate the problems and to take remedial steps before they developed. It was the concern of the congregation's ruling board that necessary staff changes be made in such a way that the pastor and his family not bear the burden of responsibility alone.

Within about nine months of joint effort, a plan was put together that allowed the pastor and the congregation to dissolve their relationship with good will. The denomination worked with the pastor to begin a new church in a rapidly growing community of his choice. The congregation provided all moving expenses and continued to pay the pastor's salary, insurance and housing until the new congregation was able to pay its own way—which wasn't very long. By the end of its first year the new congregation was averaging over five hundred in its Sunday celebration.

➡ COMMENTS In high-quality churches we often discover there is no attempt to adhere to strict universal formulas to guide a leader or a congregation when faced with dilemmas of conflicting needs or interests. This is not to deny that a church risks foundering if it does not establish ethical benchmarks for acting. A high-quality church finds flexibility within its ethical guidelines; recalling the values of the church, and with spiritual discernment, it will construct the appropriate response, given the situation.

Although this is not the place to pursue the construction of ethical values or codes, we know that such matters can be fixed within the culture of a congregation. A congregation normally starts with the Ten Commandments, then examines the social principles of the prophets of the Old Testament, followed by the teachings of Jesus and of Paul. We have not been left without a guide to help us develop a Christian ethic for our private lives and our public ministries. The prompting of the Spirit within each of us and within the congregation is consistently reminding us that "this is the way, walk in it." A discerning leader or congregation will know what is the proper decision for the situation at hand.

➡ DIAGNOSTIC QUESTIONS **Does the congregation adhere to an ethical code, distilled from, or even beyond, Scripture?** Where is the ethical code recorded? Who knows about it? How is it used?

Are the children specifically and intentionally taught how to make moral decisions? Who teaches them? How often are they taught? How many children attend these sessions? What percentage of the children attend? At what ages are the children taught ethics?

Are courses in ethics taught to adults? Who teaches the courses? How often are they taught? How many adults attend? What percentage of the adults attend?

Are ethics discussed at board or committee meetings?

Is there a clearly communicated expectation that all leaders will adhere to ethical standards when making decisions or offering leadership?

➡ IMPLEMENTATION IDEAS Courses and seminars regarding moral decision making should be offered. Many congregations recruit speakers, preferably from the congregation, to give talks about ethics in their vocational fields. For example, a general lecture on ethics might be followed by lectures on ethics in the professions: law, medicine, engineering, genetics, psychological research, government, business and so on. Ask the lecturers to compare the ethical regulations or problem situations of their professions to similar situations in the church.

In the high-quality congregation, ethical discussions are more effective when framed and presented as good news and not as bad news. This is not always possible with every biblical text. Many of the rules for living in the holiness codes of Hebrew Scripture would not be practiced by reasonable Christian communities in our culture today. But other time-worn traditions are very well received. For example, the pastor might preach a series of sermons on the ten promises of God (the Ten Commandments) by discussing them in terms of blessings that flow from obeying the conditions of God's promises to the people of God, rather than curses applied as a result of an unforgiving law. The rabbis interpret the Decalogue as God's promise of grace to Moses and the children of Israel, a promise based on a covenant relationship. It is as though God were saying, "Now, since you have been these days with me, and have come to know me better, you will no longer be bothered by these things—you will find it easier to honor your father and mother; you will not be tempted to steal from your neighbor, or to take your neighbor's spouse, etc. This series of sermons might be elucidated by the witness of laypersons who were confronted with ethical dilemmas, and how they found the grace of God sufficient to make the right decisions.

Make intentional efforts to teach ethics and values for living to children and youth. Such teaching will be more effective if it is cast in the experience of the age level being taught.

➡ **RESOURCE MATERIALS** Adams, John, ed. *Transforming Leadership: Vision to Results.* Niles River Press, 1986.

Bondi, Richard. *Leading God's People: Ethics for the Practice of Ministry.* Nashville: Abingdon Press, 1989.

Calvin, John. *Institutes of the Christian Religion.* Translated and annotated by Ford Lewis Battles. Grand Rapids: Eerdmans, 1986.

Woggaman, Philip. *Making Moral Decisions.* Nashville: Abingdon Press, 1991.

➡ EXPECTING QUALITIES

➡ ETHICAL
➡ **HAS HIGH EXPECTATIONS**

➡ DEFINITION   Having high expectations means that everyone expects a high level of commitment from clergy, staff and laity. People asked to accomplish things do so at their highest level of effort and ability. In turn, they feel respected and wanted. Having high expectations does not mean being rude or unreasonable. Persons who are demanding of themselves expect high expectations to be placed upon them, and they perform to the highest level of their abilities.

➡ EXAMPLES   At the August meeting of the church board the topic was the fall finance campaign and that so many members pledge little and give even less. "Why don't the members come through?" asked John Howe. "Our budget requests are reasonable. We don't ask that anyone give a great deal. Yet every year we have the same financial problems. Nothing seems to change. We're always short of money."

"Well," replied Nellie Green, "many of our members are retired and on fixed income. They really can't give very much. We also have a number of young families who are just getting started. We all know they don't give much but we certainly don't want to hurt their feeling by pushing them for more."

This is a conversation played out every year in thousands of congregations across America that conduct a fall pledge campaign to raise money for next year's budget.

A Young Pastor Sets a Standard of High Expectations Regarding the Church Treasury. Whenever we think of setting high expectations for a congregation, we think of Mark Blaising, currently the Area Executive Assistant to the Bishop of the Indiana Area, The United Methodist Church. When Mark was a young pastor, he was appointed to a congregation with an established reputation of financial difficulties and meager ministries. Upon his arrival he discovered that the congregation was $11,000 behind in its pledge commitments.

Mark invited the board members and lay leaders to a Saturday Morning breakfast, which he and his wife cooked and served. After the breakfast the group began to thank him and ask if they could help him pay for the food.

He said to them, "This breakfast is going to cost you more than the price of the food. You are $11,000 behind in your church budget. None of you is going to get out of this room until you contribute $50 to help make up the deficit." After everyone had produced the $50 or promised to get it to him by the next day, Mark told them that each was to go to five other members of the church that week and get $50 from each of them to help make up the deficit.

By the end of the week the $11,000 deficit had been paid. The congregation never again got behind on its budget over the several years Mark was there.

A Pastor's Plan to Lead a Congregation to Hold High Expectations of Itself in Matters of Money and Ministry. David Biebighauser is a United Church of Christ pastor in Watertown, South Dakota. Since his ordination in 1963 he has proven his ability to build quality into small and medium-size congregations by holding high expectations for his own ministry, and by consistently calling the congregation to higher expectations.

Each of the churches which he has served as pastor was long time advocates of the pledge system. In every instance, the finance committee would build the annual budget and then carry out the pledge campaign. The pledges never met the announced budget, so the finance committee would trim the budget to fit the pledges.

As the year wore on, the church board and finance committee would cut nickels and dimes out of the program budgets in order to keep the church in the black. This was always accompanied with a great deal of carping about people not taking their church obligations seriously.

David would go through his first months in each parish without saying a word about the process. Then when the first year of budget building and pledging started, with the long accustomed worries and complaints, he would state to the finance committee and boards that there is a better way to go about financing God's church. He would introduce them to the biblical standard of *tithing* and teach them to "give as the Lord has blessed you, with the tithe being your goal."

After listening to the litany of reasons why tithing would not work in *this* church, David would ask them, "Have you, as the leaders of this congregation, ever taught the people the high privilege of tithing your income to God's work, not as a law to be obeyed but as a joyful response to the many gifts God has given to each of you and your families? Have you ever set an example of tithing by doing so yourselves?"

This always led to an animated discussion, at the end of which he would challenge them to dispense with the pledging system and try at least one year of "giving as the Lord has blessed, with the tithe being your goal." He would further recommend the following: (1) Sponsor a well-planned stewardship training program; (2) develop a program budgeting and planning process; (3) allow several sermons throughout the year on biblical stewardship; and (4) if the income falls short of the budget, make up the lack by reducing his salary for the year accordingly.

In each instance the income for the year proved to be greater than the preceding year. Throughout his ministry in small- or medium-size congregations (his present church has 450 members), he would begin by challenging the congregation to undertake some hands-on goals for reaching out to the community in ways that would encourage the people to give even more money and certainly more of their personal time to ministering to the community.

The congregation he now serves has helped to organize an affiliate of Habitat for Humanity and has just dedicated their second house. The congregation helps in the financing of these homes, and builds them in partnership with the low-income families who purchase the homes at no profit and no interest. David believes that leading the congregation to have high expectations in biblical stewardship and active ministries accounts for the increased joy and vitality in the churches he has served.

In preparing David's story for this book, we visited the Sunday morning services at his church, interviewed him and conversed with members of the congregation. The people are joyful, courageous and committed to growth and service. This congregation has high expectations.

➡ COMMENTS The church that has high expectations for itself has leaders that demand the best of themselves, the members, the ministries and the programs of the church. The term *demand* does not imply a dictatorial climate in which a few persons decide what should be done and then demand that others do it. By *demand* we mean that in the high-quality congregation all persons know and feel that in private life and in public ministry the standard is: Whatever your hands find to do, do it as though you were doing it for God; as though God were right there watching you. Quality is sought in everything that the church does. Second class is not good enough.

Rather than demanding quality through policy or fiat, successful church leaders know how to "invite" it out of the people. And they begin by setting an example of unwavering commitment to quality in their own work and relationships.

In a high-quality church, laypersons are treated with respect. They are given serious tasks and are expected to carry them out in a successful and exemplary manner. Who wants to be given a "Mickey Mouse" job? Members of the laity know when they are being treated seriously. They have better things to do than waste time.

High expectations without training will short-circuit any demand for quality. It is unconscionable to demand high-level commitment of persons and not to give them the resources, skills and support needed to meet the expectations of the leaders and organization. As noted in the discussion of the quality of significant lay participation, the promise of training also makes it easier to recruit persons committed to making the effort necessary to meet the demand for quality.

We have also pointed out that it is the pastor's responsibility to give the leadership teams two types of training: general skill training and training that is targeted to the specific assignment a person is expected to fill. A system of apprentice training and a three-year rotating chairmanship are two ways to foster high expectations through training programs. The recognition programs previously mentioned would also serve well to support high expectations through lay participation.

The quality of having high expectations is linked to other qualities of being communicative and responsive, encouraging significant lay participation and listening.

➡ DIAGNOSTIC QUESTIONS **Are high expectations communicated to the clergy, staff and members?** Is the communication of the expectations done formally or informally? Is it done in writing or spoken?

Are expectations recorded?

Are expectations evaluated?

How are failures in performance dealt with?

➡ IMPLEMENTATION IDEAS Having high expectations is an attitude that must be initiated among the leadership. High expectations begin with the clergy. Unless the clergy sets the example, all efforts to meet high expectations in the congregation will likely be futile. High expectation should be taught from the pulpit. The leaders should have high expectations for themselves. These high expectations should be modeled by the leaders.

Failures should not become occasions to mete out blame and guilt. Instead, failures should be used as learning opportunities, celebrated and laid aside. New decisions and actions should then be planned, and the people encouraged to get on with it.

Each activity should establish high expectations for its leaders and participants. The food in potluck dinners should be the best in town. The paint job on the church must be perfect and use the highest-quality paints. Committees should not waste members' time. Printed programs should have no typos. (Pease, dear God, may there be no typos in this book.) It should be a delight to call the office and ask for help. This also means not calling the office when you can or should do the work yourself.

High quality does not mean acting as a spendthrift. High quality is found in a job well done—so that it lasts. A person who demands quality is not oppressive but expresses the desire to make the church a place where one is proud to be a member. When church members do things right, others will seek out and join your church.

> ➡ EXPECTING QUALITIES
>
> > ➡ ETHICAL
> > ➡ HAS HIGH EXPECTATIONS
> > ➡ **EXCELLENCE**

➡ DEFINITION   When excellence is a benchmark, all activities and behaviors of clergy and laity are performed in the best possible manner. Excellence is the attitude that enables people to do things well. Excellence, which is sometimes synonomous with quality, supports and enhances every other quality and all activities of the church. Who wants a second-rate car, meal or home? Why settle for a second-rate church?

The public recognition of problems, when followed by immediate efforts to solve the problems, is a key indicator of excellence. Excellence is mastering the ability to produce the results we truly wish to produce for God.

➡ EXAMPLES   **A Layperson Is Recognized for His Excellence in Ministry.** Consider this thrilling example of excellence at a church. A lay member was leaving the community to teach at a seminary. At the Wednesday evening New Community celebration, ten minutes was devoted to reviewing the long list of this member's services and contributions to the church. The speaker pointed out how this man had started his volunteer work at the church by picking up discarded printed programs and cups after the services during the first year of the founding of the congregation. Over the years, from this modest beginning, he became the elder in charge of pastoral counseling. His wife was also recognized for her services.

Why take ten minutes of the Wednesday evening service for recognizing this person's excellent ministry? What better way to model, before the people of God, how excellent service is desired and embodied in the life of the congregation. By such acts of recognition, the church demonstrates that dedicated ministry (volunteer and paid) is noticed and not forgotten.

Excellence: The Standard for Highly Achieving Industries. The will to be excellent is heavily dependent upon being possessed of a clear and compelling vision for the future of the church. Where there is no vision, excellence perishes. The call to aspire to excellence comes as bad news to a congregation that has long since settled for the status quo. The will to be excellent cannot be forced; it can only be found within the heart of the individual or the congregation. Excellence is, in part, a matter of spirit. The excellent corporations around the world understand this far better than do most churches and denominations.

Kazuo Inamori of Kyocera Corporation entreats his employees "to look inward," for it is there that they will discover their own internal standards. He teaches that there is a standard even greater than excellence, and that is *perfection*. And, says Inamori, perfection should be the goal. One need never settle for excellence alone. Inamori asserts that when a company (a church) strives to be excellent, its standard of measure is outside itself; the company (the church) strives to be better, and to be the best among the other companies in its field. But to aim for perfection rather than just being best will bring the company to its own internal standard, for no external standard can define perfection.

Inamori says that his vision for Kyocera is that the people will always aim for perfection, rather than just being the best. Here we see the tie that unites excellence with vision. Of vision Inamori says, "It's not what the vision is, but what it does" that matters in the life of a people or organization.[2]

Excellence: The Scriptural Standard of Performance. Many pastors and congregations have succeeded in convincing themselves that so long as Christian service is well intentioned it is acceptable, even if it might be inadequately prepared and poorly performed. This attitude, however, is not the standard that Paul sets forth in his first letter to the Corinthian church: "Do you not know that in a race all the runners run, but only one gets the prize? Run in such a way as to get the prize. Everyone who competes in the games goes into strict training" (1 Cor. 9:24-25 NIV).

This strict training is similar in attitude to our "striving for Christian perfection," which is emphasized so often in the Wesleyan tradition and is familiar to many Christians who seek to improve their holy relationship with God. Excellence in all that we are spiritually and in all that we do for God's glory as a community can be compared to our desire to become more deeply perfected, more firmly committed to "always excelling" (see 1 Cor. 15:57-58) in God's grace.

➡ COMMENTS   Excellence should happen all the time and everywhere. Even though the leaders and long-time members may be conditioned to accept shoddy preparation and lackluster performance in ministry, the people they are hoping to reach are not. Although generational theory does not explain the wants and needs of every individual, the thirty- and forty-something generation is searching for quality in religious organizations, and this generation of seekers will not stay where they do not find it.

We might deny this collective demand for high quality; we might complain about it; or we might label an entire generation as self-centered and immature, but this will not change the reality. Baby boomers are on a spiritual quest, and they are shopping for religious services with the same intensity that they exhibit when shopping for breakfast cereal in the supermarket. They will accept nothing less than the best quality for their families.

Every worker in the church should embody this pursuit of excellence. Every worker in the church should be led to ask the question, "What does it mean for me to carry out my ministry in such a way as to 'get the prize'? What does it mean for me to 'go into strict training' in order to carry out my ministry in such a way as to 'win the prize'?"

The opposite of excellence in an organization is disqualification or inferiority. All organizations tend toward atrophy, so it is no surprise that a congregation might slide into inferiority. Excellence is not achieved once but must be continually renewed. Thus no congregation can achieve excellence without tapping into the subconscious mind and imagination of the members, for excellence is an attitude of the heart before it is visible in ministry.

Within the heart, the seat of experience, is found a vital spirituality, which becomes the incubator of excellence. The reservoirs of spiritual strength, mental alertness and heart-felt commitment, which are essential to the constant quest for excellence, are tapped through spirituality and spiritual formation. Excellence is never achieved without discipline and is sometimes defined as "personal mastery" which "goes beyond competence and skills, though it is grounded in competence and skills. It goes beyond spiritual unfolding or opening, although it requires personal growth. It means approaching one's life as a creative work, living life from a creative as opposed to reactive viewpoint."[3]

Excellence should be the internal standard for every worker and program in the church; however, as lofty as it is, excellence is not the ultimate. Beyond excellence is perfection. Excellence is relative in that it is measured against the performance of others. The church that is performing best among others is doing an excellent job. However, the "best" is not the "ultimate." Perfection is measured against the possibility of being completely who God wants us to be. Beyond excellence lies the possibility of becoming perfect—in an arena where one stands alone, striving only to continue to grow into perfection.

Over the course of time, the relativity of excellence becomes more apparent to God's people as they grow in love. The competitive metaphors in Scripture about excellence come to be balanced by other affections in the divine household of faith, so that the rewards, the prizes of excellence, often appear to be tertiary and not worthy of being the primary object of our service. Church leaders discern and should not forget that God proclaims freedom and hope for the poor, the oppressed, the widow, the orphan and the captive. God is Lord of those who are sick, in pain, and who cannot fight for the prizes that are claimed by superior runners. Instead, in a congregation committed to excellence, the more ultimate focus is placed on achieving a personal best, as each individual strives for perfection. If this balance of internal and external excellence is not achieved, a congregation will unknowingly open itself up to the pride and arrogance that infect us when success is measured by bodies and bucks.

➡ DIAGNOSTIC QUESTIONS **Does the congregation do every-thing well?** How do we know people are doing things well? What meaning does the congregation attach to the phrase "doing everything well"? Do we shamelessly borrow good examples of excellent ministry from other churches?

Is there an expectation to do better then expected?

Is a process of correction initiated when an error or problem is found? Are errors and mistakes seen as opportunities to learn, or something to be punished?

Is the process of improvement continued until a satisfactory solution is reached?

Are decisions, time, energy and money directed toward exceeding current levels of accomplishment? How is the message of doing better communicated to all parties involved?

➡ IMPLEMENTATION IDEAS Both the clergy and the laity must become involved, or the drive toward excellence will not become contagious. Three steps can be implemented so that excellence becomes an effective attitude. The three steps, which presuppose the communicative quality, include: (1) motivating, (2) showing and (3) recognizing.

Several approaches may be taken to motivate a church to seek excellence. The approaches may be integrated into a comprehensive program. The mission of the church should reflect excellence. There is ample theological support for "always excelling." One might start with considering God's concern with content (we do not know the process) when God set about to create the universe. Before God ended each work, God took time to assess its content, with the desire to see that *it was good*, or, in other words, done exceptionally well. Each day of creation became a defining benchmark.

"What do people *see* when they assess our programs and efforts?" A faithful pursuit of this question will lead us all closer to excellence, and beyond—to perfection.

The minister may address the congregation with sermons (start with 1 Corinthians 15) that urge excellence as the benchmark attitude for all of the church's work. Excellence should be discussed at the highest levels of the church's leadership structures. Excellence should then become a "watchword" at all levels. Congregation meetings and symposia should be dedicated to discussing what excellence is and why it is desirable. Examples of excellence should be found and honored, and possibilities for enhancing excellence explored. It can be a game with children, but it should be a serious business for adults.

Each organization, group and individual should be asked to identify what aspects of the church's programs can be improved. In many cases, the cost of improvement will be no more than an extra minute, a single action or a timely word. In other cases, especially when congregational systems are out of control, improvement may take a long time or demand radical change. For example, improving a mediocre choir may require extensive training or money to hire soloists. On the other hand, congregation needs might be met if a mediocre choir were replaced by enthusiastic congregational singing or a few instrumental soloists. A worship team in pursuit of excellence might conclude it is better to have the choir sing once a month with excellence than to have it sing every Sunday, when the members of the choir are doing their personal best but are still ill-prepared.

For excellence to prevail, careful and intelligent standards must be adopted and understood. For example, enthusiastic singing by the congregation may not be meeting the standards of superior choral quality in a church near a university, but at many churches it would meet benchmark criteria for participation and joy. For another example, in any church, if members are observed picking up a bulletin from the sanctuary floor, or a littered paper cup in the parking lot, we know that excellence is on display.

Accomplishments and improvements should be recognized and publicly applauded. The members who repaint the hall or the computer techie who improves the church database are each contributing to excellence. Church leaders and followers should learn instinctively to comment favorably when excellence is observed.

➡ RESOURCE MATERIALS   Inamori, Kazuo. "The Perfect Company: Goal for
                        Productivity." Speech given at Case Western
Reserve University, June 5, 1985.
Diehl, William. *In Search of Faithfulness: Lessons from the Christian Community.*
  Minneapolis: Augsburg, 1987.
Peters, Thomas J. and Robert H. Waterman, Jr. *In Search of Excellence: Lessons
  from America's Best-Run Companies.* New York: Warner Books, 1982.
Senge, Peter. *The Fifth Discipline: The Art & Practice of the Learning Organiza-
  tion.* Garden City, NY: Doubleday Currency, 1990.
Shawchuck, Norman and Roger Heuser. *Leading the Congregation: Caring for
  Yourself While Serving the People.* Nashville: Abingdon Press, 1993.
Schnase, Robert. *Ambition in Ministry: Our Spiritual Struggle with Success,
  Acheivement, and Competition.* Nashville: Abingdon Press, 1993.

➡ EXPECTING QUALITIES

➡ ETHICAL
➡ HAS HIGH EXPECTATIONS
➡ EXCELLENCE
➡ **EVALUATIVE**

➡ DEFINITION   All aspects of the church should be continuously evaluated in order to improve the quality. This may be the most important and universal benchmark to be implemented in the pursuit of high quality. Good evaluation leads to the possibility of continuous improvement. It will save ministries that can perform well, but dismantle ministries that are ineffective and so out of control that they will never perform well.

➡ EXAMPLES   **Evaluation of a Choir Program Produces Life-Changing Results.** Kim Palmer is the music director in an Evangelical Free Church in California. Kim decided to conduct an evaluation of the choir experience by its members. The evaluation brought to light certain things that Kim had never before considered. For example, Kim had always assumed he and the choir members shared common goals for the choir. So he never bothered to set goals or plan the ministry with the choir.

The evaluation, however, revealed that the motives of the choir members for participating in the choir were not at all what Kim's goals were. For Kim, the goal was to present excellent choral music in the worship services of the church. For the choir members, however, the goal was to be in a cell-like community that might assist them in their spiritual journeys. The top four responses from choir members to the question about their goals:

"To be right with God and feel God's presence."
"To pray for each other and for ourselves."
"To achieve excellence and never settle for mediocrity."
"To live pure and holy lives."

This realization has completely reoriented Kim's thinking regarding his opportunities as a choir director—and it has resulted in a thorough revision of the choir program. Whereas previously the choir had merely practiced and performed, now Kim is serving as spiritual director to the members, teaching them how to rehearse with a greater attitude of worship, how to pray, how to meditate upon Scriptures and how to encourage each other through mutual healthy accountability.

"The most amazing thing about this," Kim reports, "is that almost every week one to four new people ask to join the choir, and attendance at rehearsals has increased 57 percent. We had to enlarge the choir space in the sanctuary, and attendance at the major worship services is at a ten-year high."

The evaluation model that Kim and his choir used is presented in Appendix B of *Marketing for Congregations* (Nashville: Abingdon Press, 1992).

➡ COMMENTS   The widespread absence of evaluative practices in the church is not due to a lack of skill but to a lack of courage. We know how to evaluate, but we are afraid of the results. Much of this fear can be attributed to the fact that most of the evaluations we have experienced have been for the purposes of giving a "grade" that is relative to the rest of the class, or of passing judgment on our worth. Evaluation in the church should never be used to pass judgment on people or efforts—but to *provide infor-*

mation to help the clergy, staff and congregation perform their ministries more effectively.

To overcome this natural fear, church leaders often will secure the services of a competent consultant who is able to grant permission from the outside and then freely share information that may be seized upon or rejected. The consultant always leaves town, and thus actions based on internal evaluation will require considerable courage from the church leadership, even after the initial fear subsides.

Each program or ministry unit should evaluate its work annually, and every three years the congregation should conduct a major evaluation of all its programs, ministries, and activities. In three years many programs will have already outlived their usefulness, and should either be totally overhauled or discarded to make room for new and more effective ministries. Evaluation will help in making such decisions.

➡ DIAGNOSTIC QUESTIONS   **Is evaluation accepted by staff and congregation?**

Are all activities evaluated? Who designs the evaluations? Who carries them out? What happens to the evaluations? Who sees the results? Where are they kept? Are summaries developed from time to time? To whom are the summaries distributed, and how?

Is evaluation done continuously and positively to improve all aspects of the church?

Is evaluation made a part of the structure of all activities? How is evaluation built in? Is evaluation legislated or voluntary?

➡ IMPLEMENTATION IDEAS   Evaluation, like excellence, is a frame of mind, an attitude. With each action taken, one should have an expected best outcome in mind. The leaders of the church might encourage all groups to evaluate their programs annually. A seminar in evaluation might be offered for all group leaders. The board might create an evaluation support team, whose job it is to assist other groups in designing and conducting evaluations of their programs.

Evaluation should be expected by all persons and groups who are responsible for some area of the congregation's affairs. Continuous assessment of what we are doing or what we expect from our efforts is vital. Following evaluation, active steps must be taken to nurture the successful aspects of the church's ministry, and to prune away the unsuccessful. There is no blame for failing at new ventures. The only blame is continuing to support failures or failing to support successes.

➡ RESOURCE MATERIALS Caro, Francis G. *Readings in Evaluative Research.* 2nd ed. New York: Russell Sage, 1977.

Easum, William. *The Church Growth Handbook.* Nashville: Abingdon Press, 1988. Includes a complete ministry audit.

Shawchuck, Norman, et al. *Marketing for Congregations: Choosing to Serve People More Effectively.* Nashville: Abingdon Press, 1992.

Suchman, Edward A. *Evaluation Research: Principles and Practice in Public Service and Social Action Programs.* New York: Russell Sage, 1968.

EVALUATION

Evaluation starts with listing existing activities and practices. Obtaining baseline data is critical for all evaluation. Some data can be gathered regularly, such as the amount of weekly contributions or Sunday attendance.

The first step is to collect data that can be obtained in an unobtrusive and nonreactive manner. This kind of measuring is focused on objects and on people's actions when they are not aware that they are being observed or counted, so that the observations have no perceptible effect on the persons involved in the activity being evaluated. Some examples of questions that can be answered in this way: How many cars are there in the parking lot? By what time is the parking lot filled? How many late comers arrive and at what times do they arrive? How many doughnuts are eaten during the coffee hour? How many tickets are sold for the lecture? How many inquiries about membership are received in the church office? How many bags of food are collected during the food drive?

After the data is collected, the group of evaluators should systematically look at the collected data and analyze it. The next question is, does the data speak to us, suggesting specific responses? If the parking lot is full and people are turned away, should we go to two services? Three dozen doughnuts are left over each Sunday— should we decrease the order or change to muffins and bagels? If we received only two bags of food during the food drive—surely there must be a better way to motivate members; perhaps a sermon, posters, talk it up?

Intrusive data is often needed as well. Questionnaires and interviews are intrusive and must be used with great care. One must respect the time and privacy of individuals. Questionnaires should be generally limited to two sides of one sheet. Questionnaires should not take an unreasonably long time to fill out. For example, an adult education course could have a brief questionnaire that asks about the best experience during the course, and the worse. A seven-point scale asks the respondent to rate the course between "The best course I ever had" to "No one should be subjected to the course." Quantitative data may be analyzed and open-ended questions summarized. The instructor or a committee could use the results to plan better courses.

Most church activities can be regularly evaluated, if you have the courage and care about quality. The amount and type of evaluation should be determined with due consideration for the feelings of the respondents. Good evaluation increases significant lay participation, bolsters high expectations, promotes excellence, and becomes a primary tool in the measurement of all the other qualities.

7 - Consequent Qualities

EMPLOYING THE QUALITIES DESCRIBED ABOVE LEADS TO OTHER RESULTING QUALITIES, SUCH AS HEALING, JOY, AND GROWTH.

➡ HEALING
➡ JOY
➡ GROWTH

E mploying the qualities described above leads to other resulting qualities, such as healing, joy and growth. These qualities are natural side effects of the other qualities. The qualities discussed above, working together, create a new life and spirit in the church—a spirit that is healing, joyous and expansive (or growing). One cannot program or legislate being a healing, joyous or expansive congregation.

➡ CONSEQUENT QUALITIES

➡ HEALING

➡ DEFINITION   Healing is a feeling of wholeness that leads to greater health, through relationships, worship, prayer and altered life-styles. Wounds are healed and not created, and healing is greatly aided when people live together in an integrated, healthy church environment. A healing environment develops when the qualities of being spiritual, believing, communicative, showing pastoral care and being joyous exist.

➡ EXAMPLES   The actions taken by the congregation of the First Assembly of God Church in Santa Ana, California

135

(discussed under "Participative Qualities"), to make itself vulnerable to the previously feared and shunned street gangs, has brought healing to hundreds of persons and more than a few agencies. Many church members were healed of fears and prejudices as they ministered to and related with the young people. Scores of young people have been healed of their prejudices and drug addictions. Distances between the church and governmental agencies and the Santa Ana school system have been narrowed. It is a rare and beautiful thing to see a congregation that can heal others and itself, even in the midst of its own trepidation.

This healing virtue does not develop in a vacuum. Neither does it suddenly appear "on the spot." It is the result of many of the qualities being present and acting in concert on the life of the congregations.

➡ DIAGNOSTIC QUESTIONS **Does participating in the congregation heal the physical and mental problems of members?**

Does participating in the congregation produce mental or physical injury?

Do new members come to be healed?

Do members leave the congregation with or because of hurts?

➡ IMPLEMENTATION IDEAS Self-help groups are a place for healing. Members of a church can share their pain and injury and find comfort and, at times, healing. Self-help groups may be leaderless. A basic format for a healing group should be offered; it may be led by an interested layperson, who may act as convener. Having chosen a convener and format, the group may advertise and get started. The church may conduct training events aimed at helping persons become skilled at identifying and relating to persons who are in need of healing.

From time to time, we (the authors) discover congregations that have created "healing teams," whose members may include a physician, a psychologist, a nurse, a social worker, or other persons representing healing professions. These teams of volunteers work alongside the pastors and lay leaders to consult, diagnose, structure healing routines and the like.

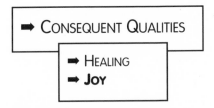

➡ Definition   When joy is present, it pervades the entire life of the congregation. It is contagious, infecting every person who relates to the congregation. Joy is expressed in the worship experiences, the business meetings, the church office and wherever the people come together.

➡ Examples   One can sense the increase of joy and authenticity of worship in the choir led by Kim Palmer. Their joyousness and genuine worship are contagious, inspiring people to join the choir and share their joy—for the joy of finding a place where they will be supported in their spiritual quest. This contagion spreads from the choir to the congregation, and without any effort attendance in the worship services begins to grow.

Many congregations are like morgues. When everyone has a long and drawn face, joy is lacking. Joy signifies a place filled with love for life. Many qualities discussed in this book support joy: significant lay participation, having many programs, being communicative, a sense of community, being responsive and excellence.

➡ Diagnostic Questions   **Are members joyful and happy?**

Do members enjoy each other and life?

Are worship, mission and education enjoyed?

Is laughter common in the congregation?

What kind of music is used in the services, songs of joy or dirges?

➡ Implementation Ideas   Joy must be modeled. It must be talked about. Persons must be given permission to be joyful.

Local and ethnic celebrations and customs that are joyful should be incorporated into the services and programs of the church. Religious and secular feast days can be major occasions of joyful fellowship in the church.

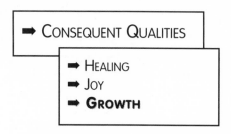

➡ CONSEQUENT QUALITIES

➡ HEALING
➡ JOY
➡ **GROWTH**

➡ DEFINIITION   To be considered a growing congregation, two conditions must be present in a church: New people continue to attend the worship, education and fellowship/personal growth activities and the base of volunteer leadership and workers consistently expands. Other useful signs of growth are increasing membership, increasing moneys to support ministries to the community, and more persons leave the parish to prepare for vocations in professional ministries. All the qualities discussed in this book will support growth.

➡ EXAMPLES   Growth can be understood at several dimensions, including attendance at services, the number of ministry program opportunities available to volunteer workers, the number of persons actively engaged in volunteer ministries, the percentage of first-time visitors who later become members or belongers, and the percentage of the annual contributions used to support ministry programs (as opposed to local and judicatory administrative costs).

Leadership Network is an organization that supports and trains pastors of large congregations. This organization suggests that to be considered growing, a large congregation must have an increase in attendance at the major worship/celebration services of at least ten percent a year, and it must expand its base of volunteer workers in ministry programs by at least five percent a year. As benchmarks of quality for growth, these percentages might not be too far off for a congregation of any size.

➡ DIAGNOSTIC QUESTIONS **What have been the observable trends in attendance, membership and participation in your church over the last year? Over the last five years?** What are the attendance patterns for the last year? If you provide more than one morning worship service, what are the attendance patterns of each service? What is attendance by age groups and by educational or ministry units?

How many members have left over the last year? The last five years? How many have left for reasons that have nothing to do with the church (moving out of town, death, etc.)? What are the reasons these people have given for leaving the church?

What have been the trends in lay leadership and volunteer ministry over the last year? The last five years? What percentage of increase/decrease has there been in volunteer ministers? How many new ministry opportunities have been created each year? Are the expectations placed on lay volunteers more demanding?

➡ IMPLEMENTATION IDEAS Constantly work to identify and remove the barriers that discourage new people from participating in the church's life and work. If the church pushes growth, decline will be the ultimate result. The way to sustain growth is not to push it, but to constantly search out and remove the barriers to growth—those conditions in the church that discourage persons from attending or joining.

To push growth causes the congregation to take an "outward" focus: Where are those people? How do we convince them to come? To concentrate on removing the barriers to growth causes the congregation to take an "inward" focus: What is there about the way we do things here that makes it difficult or discouraging for new people to visit our services and to continue attending?

Putting Quality
to Work

Quality begins with the pastor first. Quality begins with the clergy, and the compelling reasons why this is true are twofold. First, so few laypersons have ever seen a high-quality church that they do not know what to look for or how to move a church in that direction. Second, to a low-quality congregation, the idea of high quality sounds like bad news, not good news. The only power the pastor has to move a congregation toward high quality is the influence of his or her own example.

Whether we want to admit it or not, quality begins with the leaders. Quality must first be carried out *by* the pastor and applied *to* the pastor's life and work. If the clergy staff hopes to prod the laity into quality, while they, themselves, avoid and evade the assessment and accountability that quality requires, they might as well not begin the effort.

Coming as a close second, the lay ruling board must commit itself and the congregation to quality. Without the wholehearted commitment and participation of the ruling board and key lay leaders, quality will be a very hard row to hoe, to say the least.

As a paradigm for industry, quality was conceived in the post—World War II era. The concept was first introduced to the American automobile manufacturers by W. Edwards Deming, but the manufacturers were not interested. They showed Deming to the door. They already had their paradigms—style and profits. They were blind to the growing demand of Americans for quality as well as style.

Deming then introduced the concept of quality to the fledgling Japanese automobile industry in the late 1950s. The Japanese were new in the business and had no established paradigms to protect, and no set rules and regulations to blind them to the future. So they were free to adopt Deming's high-quality paradigm. In short order, all of Japan's industry rose from "junk" and "cheap" to "dependable," "desirable" and "expensive."

141

Had the American manufacturers adopted quality as their paradigm for producing and selling automobiles, they could have realized unparalleled success and profits on a worldwide scale. As it was, their former success blinded them to even greater possibilities for the future. Thus they stumbled, and soon found themselves second or third rate on the world markets.

What must be said of the American automobile industry may also be said of North American denominations and the congregations. Like the American automobile industry, the major North American denominations and their local churches experienced a season of unparalleled growth and expansion in the immediate years after World War II. This expansionist period, however, proved to be brief, lasting only two decades before the statistical indicators turned downward.

Two reasons may be put forward to explain this sudden turn of events. First, in their euphoria, the denominations focused on growth and not on removing the barriers to growth. In such instances, an organization will tend to grow for a while and then turn into decline as the internal barriers to growth "feedback" to stop the growth and to return the organization to "normal." Unless the barriers to growth are removed, no organization will have enough "energy thrust" to sustain growth indefinitely.

Second, at the fringes of the American church scene entirely new paradigms were being forged regarding what the American churchgoer and the unchurched would expect and accept from the churches they would choose to attend and support.

The so-called mainline churches, however, were oblivious to these paradigmatic shifts. Their past and present successes completely blinded them to the changes that were coming. And, more inauspiciously, even when the new paradigms for quality in worship, lay participation, and judicatory control were clearly defined, the denominations either denigrated, ignored or resisted them. Like the American automobile industry, their past successes blinded the mainline denominations to the new paradigms that were coming. They wanted to continue doing what they were already so good at, and had brought them success thus far.

Even as the mainline churches slipped into decline, a new phenomenon in American church history was being born: the nondenominational church. These congregations began springing up in every major population area in every state of the Union—and many with great success. From this phenomenon have come the mega-churches, the Vineyard congregations, the Calvary Chapels and a plethora of strong, growing congregations.

How could this happen? How could these churches thrive even as the well-established denominations faltered? The answer is painfully simple: Since they were new, they had no past successes or time-honored paradigms to protect. They were not blinded by past suc-cesses. They had nothing to lose by adopting the new paradigms that were coming.

Alongside these independent congregations and fellowships, a number of churches in every denomination managed to shrug off the old paradigms that had served them so well and adopt the new paradigms that were coming. These congregations adopted new rules and regulations for quality to guide the way they carried out their programs and ministries. They proved that quality is not the private domain of the new or the independent congregations. Thus they have reduced the barriers to growth in their place; and in spite of the fact that they are unashamedly denominational, they are flourishing.

Quality is a paradigm for carrying out the work and relationships of the church—a complete set of rules and regulations about doing things right the first time, and about not doing something until we have figured out how to do it well. Mediocrity, however, is a para-digm for just getting by.

Quality is necessary. Only the high-quality church will survive another generation, because high quality is the requirement of the new paradigm being forged by the twenty- and thirty-some-thing generations for the churches they attend. In a journal arti-cle entitled "Rough Water Ahead for Protestant Churches," The Lily Endowment reports that the baby boomers are "shopping for churches like they shop for breakfast cereal," and what they see of high quality determines where they will attend and partici-pate.[1]

The size of the church is not so important. Neither is the age of the congregation. Many small and older congregations are achieving breakthroughs into new life by adopting the high-quality paradigm.

It is generally true that the newer churches find it easier to adopt quality than the older congregations—simply because the newer churches have fewer successes to protect, less poor-quality habits to overcome, no commitments to long-standing, mediocre programs and so on. However, this should not discourage the leaders of an older congregation from adopting the high-quality paradigm. It can be done, many are doing it, and the results are well worth the effort. One way for the established congregation to move into high-quality is to install quality in new programs and with new workers, rather than to begin with existing programs and old workers, with all of their proclivities to poor quality and resistance to change.

The smaller church generally finds it easier to adopt high quality than the larger congregation. We are discovering in our studies of congregations that often a single quality decision in a small church can change everything.

We have observed repeatedly that a *kairos* moment for introducing high quality into many small congregations is when they have declined to the point of imminent closure. There is something very freeing about standing at the brink of death, because then at last the congregation has nothing to lose from discarding the old ways of doing things and adopting new standards and techniques.

Who knows? This may also prove to be true for entire denominations, who find themselves continually declining in membership. When the possibility of demise can no longer be denied, they may find the freedom to discard their old paradigms and grasp hold of the new. It is more difficult to read the warning signs for a denomination than it is for a local congregation. Nonetheless, if we look closely, we may discover signs of high-quality management already appearing in some denominations.

Two of the academies for evangelism leaders in 1993 embraced marketing as their main teaching topic.[2] One of these academies, with an attendance of over 500 Mennonite and Brethren members, conducted worship services that incorporated excellent drama and contemporary music and singing, complete with strobe lights. The message in the academies was that the environment is changing and so must the church, if it is to remain successful in its outreach ministry efforts. A few years ago, *Moody Monthly* devoted several pages to a discussion, "Is There Hope for The Methodist Church?" The general consensus of the authors was that The United Methodist Church is already showing signs of change, of new life and vitality.[3] It may be possible that the critics of the denominations are far enough removed to see signs of hope long before we can, from our up-close, insider perspective.

No denomination need decline and die. The 200-year-old American denominations need not continue on to decline and demise. They can, if they will, live at least another 200 years. One thing is sure, however: If they do live another 100 or 200 years, they will not look at all like the monolithic agencies, power structures and rules and regulations that define them today. They will need to make high quality and appropriate environmental responses a way of life. Lest we forget, *they* means *we*.

Finally, many people ask us today whether high-quality management is but another fad. We are sure it is. This fact, however, should not dissuade us from utilizing it to our advantage today, for there is an enduring set of lessons that may be learned from it and should be internalized and not forgotten.

Yes, high-quality management will likely prove to be a fad, but for our time, high-quality management will have the influence of a lasting institution. We will all do well to pay serious attention to it as long as it assists in our efforts to make the church all that it can be in our generation.

In this book, we have discussed the *content* of high quality for churches, deliberately staying away from addressing the *process* of managing quality. We chose this route because we think pastors and other church leaders already possess sufficient management skills to implement a process, once they understand the desired results of the process. In order to introduce you to the process of managing quality, we have prepared an appendix on that subject, which we hope you will find informative and inspirational.

Appendix:
Total Quality Management (TQM)

From the beginning we have noted that the bulk of the publications written on quality deal with a *process* of bringing about high quality which is often referred to as Total Quality Management. These engineering experts assume that the reader already understands the *content* of quality for his or her organization. Because of the high level of worldwide interest in Total Quality Management (TQM) among nonprofit and religious institutions, we offer this appendix to define Total Quality Management for the use of congregations as they attempt to influence the *process* of quality. We expect that other authors will soon write books advocating the process of TQM for churches. Here we will summarize and apply the key ideas for you. We have also included references to some of the important TQM books already in print. In addition, we include a section summarizing the applicable ideas from TQM to churches.

W. Edwards Deming is generally considered to be the premier pioneer of Total Quality Management. But there are other key pioneers of quality, including Philip B. Crosby, A. V. Feigenbaum, Kaoru Ishikawa, Joseph M. Juran, Taichi Ohno and Walter A. Shewart.[1]

Total Quality Management grew out of concerns with quality control at Bell Laboratories of American Telegraph & Telephone. Dr. Walter A. Shewart was the key person involved in developing the science of statistical quality control. World War II accelerated the development of quality control and applied it in the production of munitions and other materials for the war. Concern with quality, seen as the simple matter of meeting specifications, continued after the war. The great worldwide demands for American products led to an effort to meet those huge demands. Quality was often sacrificed in the rush to satisfy the insatiable demand for American goods.

In Japan under American occupation, headed by General Douglas MacArthur, Japanese industry was attempting to rebuild. Early American efforts to develop the Japanese industrial base brought

American consultants to Japan, who encouraged the Japanese to develop high-quality products.

One consequence of the American effort to rebuild Japanese industry was W. Edwards Deming's travels to Japan to teach Japanese industrialists and government officials the rudiments of Quality Management, as he had developed them. His efforts were highly successful, and the influence of W. Edwards Deming was firmly established. Two milestones in the history of Total Quality Management are the work of W. Edwards Deming and the Baldrige Award, the latter being the American embodiment of the TQM approach. We will discuss both of these below.

➡ W. EDWARDS DEMING Deming is considered the founder of the modern movement of Total Quality Management (TQM). His best-known work, of many books and

papers, is entitled *Out of the Crisis.*[2] In this book he develops his now-famous fourteen points for transforming an organization, and the seven diseases that cripple an organization. In these lists are many concepts that apply to churches. We will now take the liberty of shortening the lists to twelve points and one disease that may apply to churches. We have further inserted the key qualities that we think apply.

The twelve points should be understood and accepted by everyone in the church. The ministers and leaders

The Twelve Points of Managing a Church

1. Aim to constantly improve, serve well and grow or survive by choice (Has High Expectations, Excellence and Evaluative)
2. Adopt a philosophy that will meet your theological position and your vision (Spirituality, Discerning and Believing)
3. Do not wait for failures. Do things right the first time (Excellence, Has High Expectations)
4. Do not be cheap or sloppy. Spend the appropriate money or use the needed resources (Excellence, Has High Expectations)
5. Improve constantly and forever. You can always have a better church (Excellence, Has High Expectations)
6. Develop and use training programs for both clergy and laity (Lay-Led, Pastoral Care, Responsive)

7. Develop, use and respect professional and lay leadership (Has High Expectations, Pastoral Care, Listening)
8. Drive out fear of participation. Drive out distrust. Develop enthusiasm (Communicative, Responsive, Significant Lay Participation)
9. Break down barriers between clergy and staff, paid and volunteer, clergy and laity, as well as all other groups (Communicative)
10. Everyone is responsible for quality (High Expectations, Evaluative)
11. Encourage education and self-improvement for all. Clergy and laity should go beyond the training and development offered by the seminaries and denominations (Evaluative)
12. Transforming the church is everyone's job (Significant Lay Participation, Guided by Lay Power)

One Disease of Managing a Church

1. Having a lack of constancy of purpose.

should preach, teach and lead from these principles. Church leadership should use and teach these ideas until everyone is aboard.

It doesn't take long to bring an entire congregation on board if the leaders are thoroughly committed and preach these principles constantly. Jan Carltzen turned the Scandinavian Airlines System around in less than two years by traveling everywhere in the world where SAS employees work, and preaching to them the gospel of service for the business traveler. In a few short months SAS went from posting a multi-million dollar loss to showing a multi-million dollar profit.

Deming refused to accept fees for his 1950 lectures in Japan. The Union of Japanese Scientists and Engineers (UJSE) used the proceeds from selling reprints of Deming's lectures to establish the Deming Application Prize and Deming Prize. The Deming Application Prize became a very prestigious award for corporations with outstanding quality management programs. The Deming Prize was given to individuals who made outstanding contributions to the field of quality. Both prizes spurred the Japanese concern with quality.

Deming was not recognized in the United States until a TV news reporter and producer "discovered" him. She produced a program on the decline of American competitiveness and aired it on NBC on June 24, 1980. The program was entitled "If Japan Can . . . Why Can't We?" It catapulted Deming to fame in the United States. The program had a fifteen-minute segment covering Deming's work with the Nashua Corporation, a paper company in New Hampshire. From then on the interest in Total Quality Management and in Deming was established in the United States. Deming was active until his death in December 1993. More organizations are taking up TQM every day.

➡ THE BALDRIGE AWARD   The Malcolm Baldrige National Quality Award is another major part of the culture of TQM.[3] It was established by the U.S. Congress in 1987 and is awarded every year, if acceptable candidates are found. The award is made in three categories: manufacturing industries, service industries and small business.

The Baldrige Award has four goals:

1. Use pride of recognition and improved profitable competitiveness to stimulate American business to improve quality and productivity.
2. Recognize and use as an example companies that improve the quality of their goods and services.
3. Serve as guidelines for organizations that wish to evaluate the efforts to improve quality.
4. Develop examples and cases for companies that wish to learn how to manage for quality.

The impact of the Baldrige Award is threefold: It improves the body of knowledge on quality, improves quality education and leads to better communications between units of a company. We will again present and translate the Baldrige ideas to apply to churches.

A church, to be truly oriented to quality, should have the following characteristics:

• Have a plan for continuous improvement.
• Have a process for evaluating improvements.
• Have a plan based on comparing itself, its content, to the best churches in the world. This process is known as benchmarking.

- Have a close partnership between clergy, paid staff, laity and the community.
- Have a deep understanding of the needs of all groups served.
- Prevent errors instead of correcting them.
- Have a commitment to quality by the whole congregation.
- Simplify.
- Take charge of quality.

All parties should be committed to this process. It must be embraced by all units and used with enthusiasm.

To meet the qualifications that might be required to merit a Baldrige Award, a church would need to work on seven items:

1. *Leadership.* The clergy, paid lay staff and managing laity should be personally committed to quality. They should keep the focus on quality with all constituencies.
2. *Information and Analysis.* Members of the church would examine and improve the information available to all in order to promote quality. One would find other high-quality churches and exceed their performance. Keep track of one's performance relative to these other churches on a continuing basis. Steal shamelessly from other sources of good ideas.
3. *Strategic Quality Planning.* Have a plan to ensure quality in the long and short terms.
4. *Human Resource Development.* Develop in all members of the congregation a motivation and a skill to produce quality in all dimensions. Empower all to pursue the goals of quality in the church.
5. *Management for Quality.* Have systems in place and use them to assess and improve quality.
6. *Quality Results.* Be selective in what you measure. Provide comparisons with other churches. Be clear and specific about measurements. Explain failures in quality.
7. *Focus on Satisfaction.* Every party in the church should have their expectations met or surpassed.

The Baldrige criteria do not measure fiscal performance, innovation, environmental issues or vision development and distribution.[4] Many organizations, such as Motorola in Schaumberg, Illinois add some additional dimensions. Motorola pushes a 6 Sigma program. A 6 Sigma program means no more than three errors per million actions.

➡ **OTHER DIMENSIONS**   The Harley-Davidson company illustrates that Total Quality Management is not enough to turn an organization around. The infusion of capital spending by its parent, AMF, gave Harley-Davidson a modern plant for the turnaround. Harley-Davidson could not have survived without the additional cash to modernize facilities and equipment. After the leveraged buy out (LBO) by AMF, the management and financial confidence of a few key people kept it afloat. The confidence of Citibank personnel and others made it possible to get working capital during the tough times.[5]

Although much of the early development of Total Quality Management centered on the manufacturing sector, the service sector soon realized that TQM could be used by their organizations, even though they are different from manufacturing industries. Manufacturing is usually quite separate from the use of its product, whereas producing a service is usually inseparable from its use—and service products are highly perishable. So churches are obviously more comparable to service industries than to manufacturing industries.

Continuous improvement is one of the hallmarks of TQM. Continuous improvement in churches has four levels:

1. Developing internal quality—cleaning up your own house, doing things better
2. Developing external quality—serving better the church's many constituencies
3. Developing many qualities—healthy growth deriving from pursuing several related qualities
4. Developing new ministries—creative, new services in constant development.

By pulling together the many ideas from TQM we can again make application to churches. In summary, the principles of quality in the church are:

Put people first
Innovate all the time
Put quality in all that you do
Continually improve everything

Create a healthy environment for all; nurture and recognize each
 contributor
Be wise in using time and resources
Remember always that quality is not enough.

➡ **TQM** AT INLAND STEEL   Inland Steel Corporation has relied
on Total Quality Management in turn-
ing their business around. They have shared with us some of their
key ideas.[6]

The Inland Steel Industries Quality Policy

We believe that a relentless dedication to quality in everything we
do must be a way of life throughout Inland. It is the basis for our success. Our primary goal is to produce and provide products and services that meet or exceed our customers' expectations. Regardless of
the level of performance we have today, we know that we can and
must improve upon it tomorrow. Perfection is our ultimate goal.

Total quality applies to the work of each person in everything we
do. Each person has a customer and must view his or her performance through the customer's eyes. High quality and low cost are
compatible objectives.

Inland's Business units are committed to:

* Training, educating and motivating employees to pursue total
  quality
* Removing barriers to total quality
* Providing timely feedback on progress to quality
* Encouraging creativity and innovation
* Making decisions based on facts
* Recognizing quality improvement.

This statement with few changes could be adopted by any church.
The Inland example continues:

Our Quality Principles
* Quality is defined as exceeding customers' expectations
* Performance standards are:
  Customer satisfaction
  Doing the right things right
  On-time delivery
  Continuous improvement supported by statistical evidence
* Employees are encouraged to be fully participative
* Quality emphasizes prevention over detection of errors
* All activities support quality improvement.

Many of the same high-quality principles apply to a church. The use of statistical evidence, a large part of TQM, is less likely to be found in churches. Inland's principles continue: "The Total Quality System is made up of several independent subsystems: employee involvement, customer focus and the tools of quality."

The Total Quality System emphasizes the tools of quality: statistical measurement, charting and analysis. Instead of employee involvement, the church would consider involvement of the staff and members.

Inland uses a diagram to illustrate the continuous improvement process, shown below.

The New Quality Paradigm
* We will shift our focus from quality as something out there to the understanding that quality is in here.
* Total quality will begin not as conformance to specifications, fitness for use, or customer satisfaction, but will begin as vision, as an awareness of a creative impulse to express our vision.
* We will know the quality product and service for what it truly is—the visible and tangible expression of human excellence.

This statement is practically ready for any church. The following statements from Inland Steel are useful for any religious organization:

Vision without activity is merely a dream.
Action without vision just passes the time.
Vision with action can change the world.

The process of continuous improvement is diagrammed in the following chart.

Figure 4
The Continuous Improvement Process

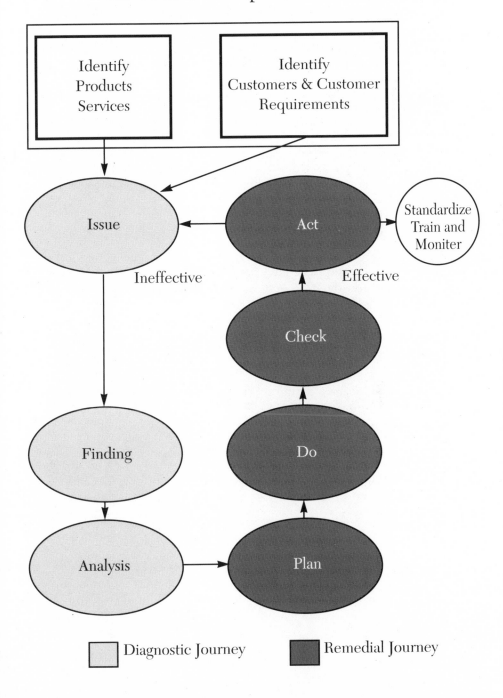

Continuous improvement starts with the identification of products and processes, while identifying customers and their requirements.

Let's suppose an issue has now developed. For example, the parking lot is full; or no one is attending the Christian history lectures.

The diagnostic journey consists of taking the issue, developing a finding about the issue and analyzing it. Once the analysis is complete, one develops a plan to carry out a solution to the problem. One carries out the plan and checks to see if it works. The act is either effective or ineffective. If effective, one standardizes the plan, trains people to carry it out, and monitors its continuing performance. If it is decided that it is ineffective, one returns to the issue and goes through the process again.

One might develop a finding that, for example, the time of the Christian history lectures is very inconvenient for potential students. Afternoon lectures are bad for adults. Monday, Wednesday, and Thursday are perceived as viable nights for the lecture series. A plan is developed to offer the lectures on Monday nights. It is implemented. Attendance is checked and the finding is that it is still unreasonably low. The issue is revisited. The finding now might be that Monday Night Football interferes with the lectures. Analyses show that Wednesday is the best night. A new series is started and it succeeds.

The Japanese have adopted a term to accentuate the need for continuous improvement: KAIZEN. Kaizen means making small improvements every day to what we are already doing well. Kaizen reminds us that it is not so much the brilliant, amazing improvement that leads us to quality as it is the constant, continuous commitment to making the small improvements day-by-day. Kaizen reminds us that there is always room for improvement. None of us has reached the pinnacle of our ministry effectiveness—there will always be room for growth and greater quality.

➡ **TQM FOR CHURCHES**   The maxims and processes encouraged by TQM can be helpful to any church. Many TQM ideas borrow from old, tried-and-true principles which you may already be practicing. At times a new fad may be used to jump start activities. In the long run the congregation's commitment to the effectiveness of the church is what counts.

KEEP KAIZENING!

KEEP KAIZENING!

KEEP KAIZENING!

KEEP KAIZENING!

Notes

Why Quality Is So Important

1. Dallas Willard, The Spirit of the Disciplines (New York: Harper & Row, 1990).

2. Henri Nouwen, *The Living Reminder: Service and Prayer in Memory of Jesus Christ* (New York: Harper & Row, 1984).

3. Carlo Carretto, *Letters to Dolcidia*, ed. Gian Carlo Sibilia, trans. Michael J. Smith (Maryknoll, NY: Orbis Books, 1991).

4. Lyle Schaller, *The Seven-Day-A-Week Church* (Nashville: Abingdon Press, 1992), pp. 72-75.

5. Kenneth A. Briggs, "Baby Boomers: Boom or Bust for the Churches?" *Progressions* 2, 1 (January 1990).

6. Based on an interview with Professor Donald F. Frey of the Department of Industrial Engineering, Robert R. McCormick School of Engineering and Applied Science, Northwestern University. Professor Frey was a senior executive in the Ford Motor Company during the 1960s.

7. See the example set forth in the building of the Temple at Jerusalem (1 Kings 6), in the exhortations to pastors (Jeremiah 23; Ezekiel 34), in the example of Christ throughout the Gospels, and in the teachings of Paul, quoted earlier in this chapter.

8. For an in-depth discussion of this principle, see Peter M. Senge, *The Fifth Discipline* (New York: Doubleday Currency, 1990), pp. 95ff.

9. Norman Shawchuck, Philip Kotler, Bruce Wrenn, and Gustave Rath, *Marketing for Congregations: Choosing to Serve People More Effectively* (Nashville: Abingdon Press, 1992).

Religious Qualities

1. The Means of Grace is a collection of spiritual disciplines that Jesus modeled in his own life, and that the reformers taught as essential to the Christian life. John Wesley taught the means of grace to be prayer, searching the Scriptures, fasting, the Lord's Supper, spiritual conversation, acts of mercy, and avoiding doing harm to others. The vital doctrines as taught by John Wesley included prevenient grace, convicting grace, saving grace, justifying grace, and sanctifying grace.

2. For further discussion of the quality of being vision led, see Norman Shawchuck and Roger Heuser, *Leading the Congregation: Caring for Yourself While Serving the People* (Nashville: Abingdon Press, 1993). Also see Shawchuck et al., *Managing the Congregation*, by same authors (forthcoming, Abingdon Press).

3. Guy Kawasaki, *Selling the Dream* (San Francisco: HarperCollins, 1991), pp. 62-63.

4. Alvin Lindgren and Norman Shawchuck, *Management for Your Church: How to Realize Your Church's Potential Through a Systems Approach* (Leith, ND: Spiritual Growth Resources, 1977), pp. 45-59.

5. For a complete discussion of the Nominal Group Technique and of the Delphi process, see Andre Delbecq et al., *Group Techniques for Program Planning: Nominal Group Techniques and Delphi Process* (Green Briar, Madison, WI. 1986).

6. David Lonsdale, *Listening to the Music of the Spirit: the Art of Discernment* (New York: Ava Maria Press, 1992).

7. For information on St. Ignatius's discernment method, contact Jesuit Sources, Fusz Memorial Building, University of St. Louis, St. Louis, Missouri. Ask for the Assistancy Seminar booklets on discernment.

8. For a brief study into Ignatian discernment as it is practiced today, see the small booklets identified above.

9. Joseph Cardijn, *Laymen into Action* (London: Geoffrey Chapman, 1964).

10. Ibid.

11. Robert Schlosser, *Miracle in Darien* (Logos International: Plainfield NJ, 1979).

Lay-Led Qualities

1. Inside-out thinking is the kind of thinking that goes on when the church leaders think they know what is best for the members and the people the church is trying to reach. The leaders make all the decisions for the members and those whom they wish to serve inside the board room, and then announce them to the people "out there." This is the opposite of Outside-in thinking, in which the leaders make serious attempts to get outside of the board room and into the minds of the members and those they are trying to serve in order that they might understand the needs and interests of the people—and then make decisions based on what they are hearing and learning.

2. See Shawchuck et al., *Marketing for Congregations.*

Gathering Qualities

1. Schaller, *The Seven-Day-A-Week Church,* p. 74.

2. Mark Blaising served Trinity United Methodist Church in Elkhart from 1975 until 1986. During his tenure, the congregation grew from 1,200 to 1,590 members, 400 to 590 in Sunday attendance, and from 183 average in church school to an average of 389 eleven years later. During these years the congregation launched more than 50 ministry opportunities for its members and other interested persons.

3. See Lyle Schaller, *Strategies for Change* (Nashville: Abingdon Press, 1993).

Participative Qualities

1. See Martin Marty, *Context* 25, 8 (April 15, 1993).

Expecting Qualities

1. The Better Preparation for Ministry Project, a research study recently conducted by McCormick Theological Seminary, found that more than anything else, congregations desire integrity in their pastors. Indeed, the top seven items identified tended to deal with the person of the pastor.

2. Kazuo Inamori, "The Perfect Company: Goals for Perfection." Speech given at Case Western Reserve University, Cleveland, Ohio, June 5, 1985.

3. Peter Senge, *The Fifth Discipline: The Art and Practice of the Learning Organization* (New York: Doubleday Currency, 1990).

Putting Quality to Work

1. "Rough Waters Ahead for Protestant Churches," The Lily Endowment, *Progressions,* Vol. 2, No. 1, 1990—Baby Boomers: Boom or Bust for the Churches, p. 4.

2. The National Evangelism Leader's Academy is sponsored by the Mennonite Church, the Mennonite Brethren Church, the Church of the Brethren, The Christian Church. The Academy meets in several locations across North America each year and is open to all who wish to register. For more information, contact Paul Mundy, Church of the Brethren, national offices Elgin, Illinois.

3. "Is There Hope for the Methodist Church?" *Moody Monthly.* Methodist on the Mend—Philip Harrold March 1991, Vol. 91, No. 7, p. 58.

Appendix: Total Quality Management (TQM)

1. See Jerry Bowles and Joshua Hammond, *Beyond Quality* (New York: G. P. Putnam's Sons, 1991).

2. See W. Edwards Deming, *Out of the Crisis* (Cambridge, Mass.: MIT Center for Advanced Engineering Study, 1986).

3. Christopher Hart and W. L. Bogan, *The Baldrige* (New York: McGraw-Hill, 1992).

4. Bowles and Hammond, *Beyond Quality*, pp. 144-47.

5. Peter C. Reid, *Well Made in America: Lessons from Harley-Davidson on Being the Best* (New York: McGraw-Hill, 1990).

6. Excerpts taken from a talk by David Byrne, Director of Management and Organizational Development of Inland Steel Industries at Northwestern University, May 18, 1993.

Index

Index of Scripture References

Old Testament

New Testament